D1392545

For Beginners LLC
62 East Starrs Plain Road
Danbury, CT 06810 USA
www.forbeginnersbooks.com

Text Copyright: © 1995 Donald D. Palmer
Illustration Copyright: © 1995 Donald D. Palmer
Cover & Book Design: Terrie Dunkelberger

This book is sold subject to the condition that it shall not, by way of trade or otherwise, be lent, re-sold, hired out, or otherwise circulated without the publisher's prior consent in any form of binding or cover other than that in which it is published and without a similar condition being imposed on the subsequent purchaser.

All rights reserved. No part of this publication may be reproduced, stored in a retrieval system, or transmitted in any form or by any means, electronic, mechanical, photocopying, recording, or otherwise, without prior permission of the publisher.

A For Beginners® Documentary Comic Book
Originally published by Writers and Readers, Inc.
Copyright © 1997

Cataloging-in-publication information is available from the Library of Congress.

ISBN-10 # 1-934389-15-3 Trade
ISBN-13 # 978-1-934389-15-7 Trade

Manufactured in the United States of America

For Beginners® and Beginners Documentary Comic Books® are published by For Beginners LLC.

Reprint Edition

SARTRE

FOR BEGINNERS

WITHDRAWN

TABLE OF CONTENTS

WITHDRAWN
Short Loan Collection

WHO IS JEAN-PAUL SARTRE?

Jean-Paul Sartre

(1905-1980) virtually held court over French intellectual life for twenty years. He influenced writers, artists, social scientists, and political activists around the world.

(NOT TO MENTION THE THOUSANDS OF UNIVERSITY STUDENTS AND DROP-OUTS IN SCORES OF COUNTRIES WHO SAT AROUND IN COFFEE HOUSES, DRESSED IN BLACK, THINKING MELANCHOLY THOUGHTS IN HIS NAME.)

He was one of the most famous philosophers of his century, as well as an influential novelist, playwright and political activist; yet he was never satisfied with his own intellectual views.

He put the name

"existentialism"

on the philosophical map, only to abandon existentialism for

Marxism.

THEN, FINALLY, HE ABANDONED MARXISM TOO.

A thorn in the side of the French government, he was so popular that, at his death, 50,000 people followed his funeral cortege through the streets of Paris.

WHO WAS THIS MAN?

J ean-Paul Sartre was born in Paris on June 21, 1905. His mother's family was from Alsace-Lorraine, the section of eastern France whose natives speak both French and German, and over whose borders France and Germany had been quarreling for years.

Jean-Paul's mother was a first cousin of **Albert Schweitzer** (1875-1965), the German theologian, missionary, and musicologist.

Jean-Paul's father died when Sartre was only a year old. His mother sought solace in her little son and concentrated all her attention on him. She moved back to her parent's home, where Jean-Paul's grandfather became a stern influence on him. When he was twelve years old his mother remarried. The spoiled "Poulou," as she had nicknamed him, experienced her marriage as a loss and a betrayal.

Nooo...!

I mmediately afterward he decided that God did not exist—though his grandfather and his stepfather definitely did exist. (Sartre spent the next 63 years rebelling against them.)

Unfortunately he was not a very good-looking kid. He was pimply, had a strabismus (a wandering eye) due to an illness when he was four years old,

and he was short—5 feet 3 inches tall. (Nevertheless, that made him a half-inch taller than his father had been.)

At seventeen, Jean-Paul received his "baccalaureate" (an elite high school diploma) and began a six-year study at the Sorbonne for his "agrégation," the exam that would be a ticket to an academic career in philosophy.

HEY! IT COULD'A BEEN WORSE! THE CLASS COULD'A BEEN BIGGER!

SURPRISINGLY, IN 1928 HE FAILED HIS "AGRÉGA-TION," COMING IN LAST IN HIS CLASS.

LAST IN HIS CLASS

MAYBE YOU COULD GET RID OF THE BUN?

Luckily, this delay in his academic career resulted in his meeting a young philosophy student named **Simone de Beauvoir**, who was smart, beautiful, nice to Sartre, and (important!) not taller than he.

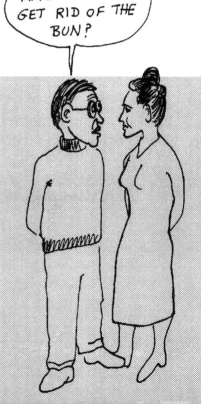

They fell in love and developed a companionship that would last until he died— even though they never married, preferred not to live  lives. They philosophized together and deeply influenced each other's work. Scholars are still sorting out who was the more original thinker. Today their ashes together, had other lovers, and addressed each other with the formal "vous" throughout their are buried next to each other in the Montparnasse Cemetery in Paris.

Jean-Paul and Simone studied together for the "agrégation." In the evenings they would go together to see cowboy films. Sartre got first place in the exam; de Beauvoir got second place.

In 1929, Sartre began eighteen months of obligatory military service. When he was discharged, he was offered a teaching job at a lycée (a type of state-run prep school for students selected to continue on to university) in Le Havre on the northwest coast of France. De Beauvoir took a teaching job at a lycée in Marseilles on the southern coast. They managed to meet each other whenever they could.

At one of these meetings in Paris, Jean-Paul and Simone were drinking beer at a bistro with their friend, Raymond Aron, who had been studying the philosophy of "phenomenology" in Germany, when Aron turned to Sartre, saying, "You see, my little friend, if you're a phenomenologist, you can talk about this drink and that's philosophy."

Sartre got very excited about the idea of being able to philosophize about his glass of beer, so in September of 1933 he went to Berlin to study the philosophy of Edmund Husserl, the founder of "phenomenology." (We'll talk about this philosophy shortly.) He returned to his teaching job the next year and began incorporating his newly-discovered phenomenological insights into his own writings. (In fact, in his novel *Nausea*, published in 1938, there is a phenomenological analysis of a glass of beer.)

But beer was not the only source of Jean-Paul's "highs." In February of 1935, he had his first experience with the drug mescaline.

> *IT MUST HAVE BEEN A "BAD TRIP," BECAUSE FOR THE NEXT YEAR AND A HALF I BELIEVED I WAS BEING CHASED BY A LOBSTER.*

These years just before the outbreak of World War II were productive ones for Sartre. In addition to his successful novel, *Nausea*, he also wrote two philosophy books: *The Psychology of the Imagination* (1936) and *Transcendence of the Ego* (1937).

But the peace ended on September 3, 1939, when France and Britain declared war on Germany. Sartre was re-inducted into the army.

His division was sent to Eastern France, where he worked in the meteorological service sending up balloons, testing the direction of the wind. However, the war interfered little with his own productivity: he began a big novel, *The Age of Reason* (published in 1945), and read the nineteenth-century Danish philosopher, Søren Kierkegaard.

HE NEVER SAW AN ENEMY SOLDIER UNTIL THE DAY HE WAS TAKEN PRISONER ON JUNE 21, 1940.

In the prisoner of war camp, he washed rarely, didn't shave, and developed a reputation for being dirty. In these conditions he began writing a major philosophical work, *Being and Nothingness* (published in 1943).

In March 1941, he escaped from the Stalag, sneaked back to Paris, and returned to a teaching job that he had started there just before the war. With some other intellectuals he formed a resistance group called "Socialism and Liberty,"

but dissolved it after a few months, having accomplished very little.

Sartre then contributed articles to underground newspapers, putting himself in some danger, and he wrote a play called *The Flies,* which contained a blatant anti-Nazi message. The play opened in June 1943 and ran for forty performances. Even though uniformed Nazis attended the play, it was not suppressed.

BRAVO

DeBEAUVOIR   SARTRE   CAMUS   PICASSO

When Sartre was not writing, he was spending time in Parisian cafés with de Beauvoir and other writers and artists such as Albert Camus and Pablo Picasso.

The ideas in his plays, novels, and philosophy books had struck a cord in Parisian intellectual life. Suddenly existentialism was in vogue and Sartre was famous. He was invited around the world to lecture. His ideas were also spread through his editorship of a new prestigious journal, *Les Temps Modernes* (Modern Times), named after Charlie Chaplin's movie.

WHEN THE WAR FINALLY ENDED IN 1945, SARTRE FOUND HIMSELF A CULT FIGURE.

DURING THIS PERIOD HE FELL UNDER THE POLITICAL INFLUENCE OF THE PHILOSOPHER MAURICE MERLEAU-PONTY AND BEGAN A RAPID MOVE TO THE LEFT.

Ironically, his political movement toward Marxism meant he was being pulled away from existentialism at the very moment that he was famous because of it.

HALLELUJAH, I HAVE SEEN THE LIGHT!

He abandoned his promised sequel to *Being and Nothingness* because he had "converted" (his word) to Marxism, yet he refused to join the French Communist Party. Nevertheless, in the "Cold War" he aligned himself against the United States and with the Soviet Union, which he visited frequently.

Sartre's defense of the U.S.S.R. caused a split between him and his fellow existentialist, Albert Camus.

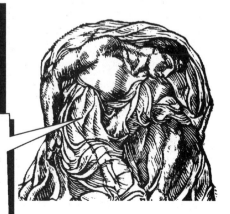

YET SARTRE, TOO, WAS SHOCKED BY THE BRUTALITY WITH WHICH THE SOVIETS REPRESSED THE UPRISING IN HUNGARY IN 1956.

13

By the late 1950s, a new intellectual style called "**STRUCTURALISM**" was stealing the thunder from existentialism, but Sartre was too deeply involved in his political projects to defend himself against structuralism, and, in any case, he had moved further away from existentialism by then. In 1960, he published Volume One of his Marxian work, *The Critique of Dialectical Reason*. As we will see, even though in it he condemned his earlier ideas, he was still

CLAUDE LÉVI-STRAUSS STEALS SARTRE'S THUNDER

influenced by them enough to try to rescue the individual and freedom from the kind of monolithic Marxism represented by Stalinism and the French Communist Party. He promised Volume Two of the *Critique* in a year, and worked on a massive manuscript that he finally abandoned. (It was published in French in 1985, five years after his death.)

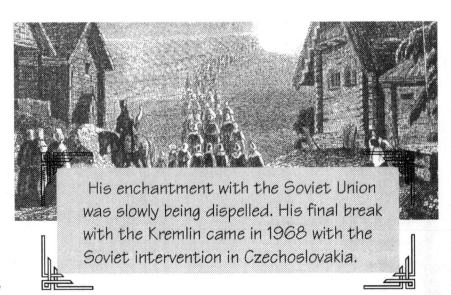

His enchantment with the Soviet Union was slowly being dispelled. His final break with the Kremlin came in 1968 with the Soviet intervention in Czechoslovakia.

KILL SARTRE!
KILL SARTRE!

He nevertheless continued his Leftist political activities. Because he sided with the native Algerians in the French war in Algeria, 5,000 army veterans marched down the Champs-Elysées chanting "Kill Sartre," who was forced to go into hiding. When his apartments were discovered, two bomb attacks ensued.

In 1964, Sartre was awarded the Nobel Prize for literature, which he rejected on political grounds. During the sixties he vigorously supported the Cuban Revolution (he finally broke with Fidel Castro in 1971), and he joined the 92-year-old Bertrand Russell's tribunal to investigate American war crimes in Vietnam.

OK, BUT REMEMBER, NO MORE FREE CIGARS!

When in 1968 the streets of Paris were filled with students in rebellion, Sartre supported the students and, in fact, was blamed by the right-wing press for causing the revolt. He condemned the Conservative government of President de Gaulle for oppressing the young and attacked the French Communist Party for betraying what he thought was a true revolution.

The demonstrations in Paris marked a watershed in his life. He never wore a suit or tie again, not even on formal occasions. Despite supporting radical political groups throughout the seventies, by 1977 he was forced to say:

> I AM NO LONGER A MARXIST.

During this decade, the abuse to which he had submitted himself during much of his life took its toll on his health. (He drank too much whisky, he smoked two packs of cigarettes a day, and he took drugs to "rev" himself up when he wrote philosophy.)

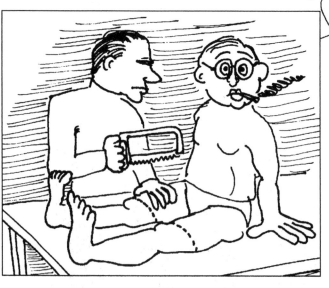

His doctor threatened to amputate first his toes, then his feet, then his legs, if Sartre would not give up smoking. Sartre said he would consider it. By the end of his life he was almost blind.

Jean-Paul Sartre died on April 15, 1980. Physicians had to dissuade the distraught Simone de Beauvoir from spending the night lying on top of his body. Even though his intellectual status had been eclipsed by the success of structuralism and post-structuralism, he was still immensely popular personally at the time his death. The streets of Paris teemed with people honoring him on his final journey to the cemetery.

EXISTENTIALISM

Despite the fact that in later life Sartre drifted away from existentialism, he established his first fame as an existentialist, and it is very likely that he will be best remembered for it.

WHAT IS EXISTENTIALISM?

EXISTENTIALISTS? OR PEOPLE WITH AN ATTITUDE PROBLEM?

Many people claim that it cannot be defined, that it is more of a shared mood than an identifiable philosophy; and indeed those who have been called "existentialists" certainly are a motley crew.

For example, there seems to be no religious or political common denominator. Sartre recognized two nineteenth-century thinkers as proto-existentialists, the Dane **SØREN KIERKEGAARD** (1813-1855) and the German **FRIEDRICH NIETZSCHE** (1844-1900). Yet the former was a deeply committed Christian and the latter a rabid atheist.

> ALMOST LITERALLY "RABID." HE SPENT THE LAST YEARS OF HIS LIFE IN AN INSANE ASYLUM.

> WHAT TIME IS IT? 3 O'CLOCK? THEN GOD EXISTS, AND MARY IS HIS MOTHER.

The Spanish Basque philosopher **MIGUEL DE UNAMUNO** (1864-1936) was a Catholic, or an atheist, or an agnostic, depending on what time of day you asked him.

> THERE ARE NO CATHOLIC EXISTENTIALISTS

> RIGHTTTTTT

Sartre's compatriot **GABRIEL MARCEL** (1889-1973) was calling himself an existentialist when the Pope announced that there were no Catholic existentialists.

FRANZ KAFKA (1883-1924) and MARTIN BUBER were Jewish and Fydor Dostoevsky (1821-1881) was Russian Orthodox.

There is almost as much political divergence as there is religious variety among those who have been called "existentialists."

KIERKEGAARD was conservative,
NIETZSCHE was anti-political,
ALBERT CAMUS (1913-1960) and KARL JASPERS
(1883-1969) were political liberals,
MARTIN HEIDEGGER (1889-1976) was once a
member of the Nazi Party,

and Unamuno was either on the Left or the Right, depending on what day you asked him.

WHAT DAY IS IT? TUESDAY? THEN I'M A RIGHT-WINGER. ¡VIVA FRANCO!

With such amazing variation on these and other topics, how is a common denominator to be found that is strong enough to serve as a unifying definition?

Jean-Paul Sartre himself (who, after all, coined the term "existentialism") has offered a definition in his essay of 1946, "Existentialism Is a Humanism."

According to Sartre, an existentialist is someone who believes and acts upon the following proposition as it applies to human beings:

EXISTENCE PRECEDES ESSENCE.

What does that mean?

Well, consider the opposite view—that

ESSENCE PRECEDES EXISTENCE.

"Essence" here means any or all of these:

 What a thing is.

 A thing's definition.

 The idea of a thing.

 A thing's nature.

 A thing's function.

 A thing's "program."

ow, we might say that in the case of artifacts, essence does indeed precede existence. Imagine the invention of scissors:

Here, the **IDEA** of the thing precedes the actual creation of the object. (The opposite would be rare.)

Also, notice that the **VALUE** of the object depends on how well the object conforms to its "idea" (to its function). Scissors that won't cut paper are BAD scissors; or perhaps they are not scissors at all.

It could be said of nature, too, that its essence precedes its existence.

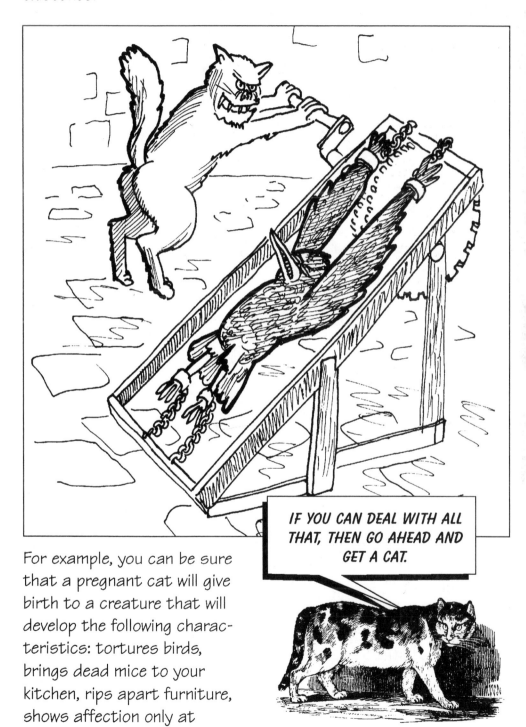

IF YOU CAN DEAL WITH ALL THAT, THEN GO AHEAD AND GET A CAT.

For example, you can be sure that a pregnant cat will give birth to a creature that will develop the following characteristics: tortures birds, brings dead mice to your kitchen, rips apart furniture, shows affection only at mealtime.

Now, according to Sartre, the Western philosophical tradition from Socrates forward has dealt the same way with humans,

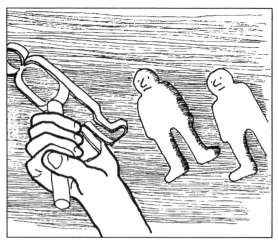

essence that stamps out individual humans like a cookie-cutter, or in the sense that the idea of the human being exists in God's mind prior to

believing that their "essence precedes their existence"— either in the sense that there is some pre-existing Platonic God's creation (very much the way in which the idea of the scissors existed in the mind of the inventor).

WHAT I NEED IS A LITTLE ONE SOMETHING LIKE ME.

WHY?

POP

In this conception, humans, like scissors, are evaluated in terms of their correspondence to their essence. A human who does not meet the pre-established criteria is a <u>bad</u> human, or maybe not a human at all. But for Sartre, all this ended in the nineteenth century when Nietzsche announced the bad news (or for Nietzsche the <u>good</u> news):

GOD IS DEAD.

We could say, figuratively speaking, if there is no God, then there is no idea in God's mind to which the human must correspond.

Or, as Sartre says:

Each human being is alone, "abandoned," and free. Each human being creates and re-creates his or her "essence" in every moment through his or her choices and actions.

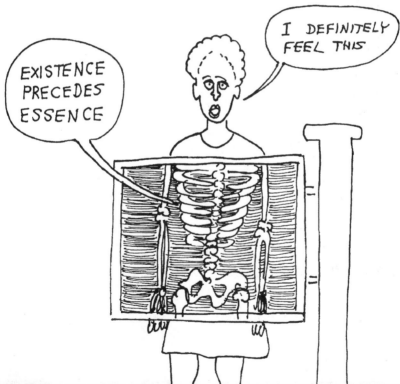

If you believe this, and "feel it in your bones," you are an existentialist.

In a certain sense, Sartre's definition of existentialism simply radicalizes a view that is very common among most social scientists: that there are no <u>instincts</u> that cause specific actions.

IN THIS WAY, HUMANS ARE VERY UNLIKE CATS.

HEY! SHUT UP!

LOOK, I DON'T REALLY WANT TO DO THIS. I CAN'T HELP MYSELF

In the case of behavior produced by true instincts, there are no alternatives. (Trap-door spiders <u>must</u> weave trap doors, and warblers <u>must</u> warble.) It is true that there are human bodily functions and reflexes that work on this model of <u>necessity</u> rather than on a model of freedom, but they never produce true human ACTIONS.

THINK OF THE DIFFERENCE BETWEEN A **BLINK** AND A **WINK** TO GET THIS POINT.

Even biological "drives" like nutrition and sex are not INSTINCTS, because the demands they make are met through culturally sanctioned actions involving intention and choice.

PURSUING THE NUTRITIVE DRIVE

There are always alternatives to anything that counts as a human action. As we will see, for Sartre, this is always true, even when we <u>feel</u> that there are no alternatives.

_O_ne last point concerning Sartre's formula, "existence precedes essence": It might seem that, according to this definition, an existentialist would necessarily be an atheist.

YET WE HAVE SEEN THAT A NUMBER OF INDIVIDUALS WHO HAVE BEEN CALLED EXISTENTIALISTS ARE RELIGIOUS.

Indeed, the acknowledged founder of existentialism, Søren Kierkegaard, was a radical Christian. Of course, he did not deny that God existed, nor that humans were God's creation, but Kierkegaard claimed that a belief in God could only be that—a <u>belief</u>, an article of faith grasped passion- ately, and never a scientific datum nor a logical deduction. For him, there was an "infinite abyss" between the human and God.

THE INFINITE ABYSS

God had left us "in absolute isolation" (like Sartre's abandonment): When we call out to God, we are greeted by a massive silence. For Kierkegaard, that silence <u>is</u> God's presence. We are, says Sartre (paraphrasing Kierkegaard), like the jetsam and flotsam left on the sandy beach, and the roar of the receding tide is like the silence that is God.

THE JETSAM AND FLOTSAM ON LIFE'S BEACH

In emphasizing our abandonment, and the freedom God has given us—and therefore our responsibility for ourselves—Kierkegaard is saying that, in turning to God, we are turning to our own freedom.

Therefore, for Kierkegaard, too, human existence precedes its essence.

PHENOMENOLOGY

If the content of Sartre's early philosophy is called "existentialism," its method is called "phenomenology." In fact, his main work, *Being and Nothingness* (1943), is subtitled, "An Essay in Phenomenological Ontology." "Ontology" is the study of Being, of Reality.

But what is PHENOMENOLOGY?

It is the name of the technique that I employ, and you will have to come to grips with it before you can deal with the detail of my theory.

Phenomenology was the creation of the German philosopher **EDMUND HUSSERL** (1859-1938), an older contemporary of Sartre whose ideas Jean-Paul studied in Germany.

But before we can deal with Husserl, we'll have to go back even further in time to Husserl's inspiration, the French philosopher **RENE′ DESCARTES** (1596-1650), who inaugurates modern philosophy with his pronouncement

I THINK, THEREFORE I AM

MON DIEU, WHAT HAVE I STARTED NOW?

With that assertion, Descartes moved consciousness to center stage. Several implications follow from this move:

Consciousness is that which is most certain. It cannot be doubted. (Even wondering if you have a mind proves that you *do* have one.)

We know consciousness better than we know the physical world (because when we know material bodies, we know them through consciousness).

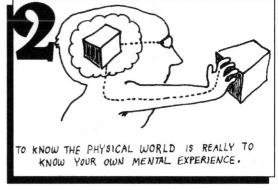

TO KNOW THE PHYSICAL WORLD IS REALLY TO KNOW YOUR OWN MENTAL EXPERIENCE.

From the fact that you think, you can deduce with certainty that you exist.

Descartes concluded, then, that all knowledge would have to be derivable from the certainty of consciousness, and all science would have to be built upon that certainty.

This was an auspicious beginning for consciousness. Unfortunately, however, by the beginning of the twentieth century, things had not gone so well for consciousness. Freud had demoted it,

Marx had trashed it;

> WE ARE ONLY INTERESTED IN THE UNCONSCIOUS. THAT IS, IN THAT WHICH IS NOT IN CONSCIOUSNESS.

> CONSCIOUSNESS IS MERELY FALSE CONSCIOUSNESS.

social scientists were ignoring it,

and the new behavioristic psychology of John Watson (1878-1958), forerunner of B.F. Skinner, denied it existed at all. Indeed, even those psychologists who believed in it and looked for it (like Herman von Helmholtz [1821-1894]), had trouble finding it.

Try this experiment: Quiz seven people about what they see in their "mind's eye" after hearing this sentence:

"THE SOLDIERS CHARGED DOWN THE HILL LIKE A HERD OF STAMPEDING BUFFALO."

BUFFALO ON GRASS

BUFFALO IN DUST

SOLDIERS ON GRASS

SOLDIER RIDING BUFFALO

SOLDIERS IN DUST

SOLDIER WITH BUFFALO

Chances are, you'll get seven completely different answers.

HALF-SOLDIER, HALF BUFFALO

Yet all seven people understood the sentence. Therefore, say the critics of consciousness,

what goes on in "consciousness" obviously doesn't matter to "understanding."

But Edmund Husserl disagreed. What was needed, he thought, was a METHOD that would display the subjective features of consciousness, as well as its objective structure. This, then, is what phenomenology is supposed to achieve.

ONLY I CAN HAVE MY HEADACHE.

NOT TONIGHT, DEAR, YOU HAVE A HEADACHE.

There are two stages in its development. The first simply involves a careful and detailed description of the way that the world presents itself to consciousness in all of its textures, excesses, and subtleties.

THE SECOND LEVEL IS MORE TECHNICAL.

Its goal is the establishment of a pre-theoretical description of the various acts of consciousness and their objects. It is pre-theoretical because it is meant to produce a DESCRIPTION of the various acts of consciousness, not a THEORY of consciousness. (Theories of consciousness always contain references to purely theoretical entities not actually present in consciousness, such as Freud's "unconscious," or the neurons and synapses in theories about how the brain causes consciousness.)

WAIT A MINUTE! IF I'M NOT CONSCIOUS OF THE UNCONSCIOUS, HOW DO I KNOW THAT IT EXISTS?

It is meant to be assumption-free, because assumptions are things presupposed by conscious states, but not in conscious states.

THINK HOW MANY ASSUMPTIONS THERE ARE BEHIND EVERY MENTAL STATE.

DENK ICH, DAFOR BIN ICH

For example, as a college student goes to her class, she assumes but does not consciously think that everyone else in the class will be wearing clothes, that the professors and the students will face each other, and be speaking English rather than, say, Yiddish.

This goal of disposing with assumptions is achieved by what Husserl calls a "phenomenological suspension," or "bracketing," or using a Greek word related to "suspension"—an "epoché."

Consciousness gets "bracketed off "from the rest of the world. What gets suspended in consciousness is its normal relation to "the world":

YOUR MONEY OR YOUR LIFE!

WHAT'S THIS GOT TO DO WITH ME?

(To see something as a pen is to see it for writing. To see gestures is to interpret them as friendly or menacing.)

The aim is to achieve something as close to an "innocent eye" as is possible, which is perhaps why children are more naturally "phenomenological" than adults.

(For example, kids often enjoy hanging their head out of the car window just to watch the broken line in the road appear to rush at them like blasts from a ray-gun.)

We can perform an epoché on any conscious experience, bracketing it, describing it in detail while trying to make as few judgments and have as few assumptions and expectations as possible.

If we bracket our consciousness of TIME, we discover, according to Husserl, that time is experienced at two levels—"clocked" time and "lived" time. The former is a cultural overlay that we must teach to our children, and into which we, as adults, become absorbed.

The latter is time as it is actually experienced prior to any acculturation or abstraction. We discover that at the level of "lived time" there is an eternal

ARE YOU HUNGRY?

I DON'T KNOW. LET ME CHECK.

NOW.

This is the way infants and children experience time before we force "clocked time" on them.

RECALL THE WONDERFULLY LONG WARM SUMMER AFTERNOONS OF CHILDHOOD PLAY, INTERRUPTED ONLY BY MOMMY'S CALL THAT IT WAS TIME TO GO IN.

Similarly, the phenomenological analysis of SPACE reveals that beneath "mapped space" there is "lived space"— a ubiquitous HERE relative to which everything else is THERE in various degrees of "thereness." In fact, according to Husserl, the HERE/NOW experience is the phenomenological ground-zero of all consciousness. Husserl tried to derive a "pure ego," an "absolute self," from the phenomenological study of pure consciousness-very much as Descartes had deduced selfhood from consciousness three hundred years earlier with his "COGITO ERGO SUM."

DARLING, I LOVE TO BE WITH YOU

BUT YOU ARE STILL OVER **THERE**

In this short book of 1937, Sartre uses the phenomenological method to inspect consciousness, but he reaches results quite distinct from those of Edmund Husserl. Let us start by defining two of Sartre's phenomenological terms: unreflected consciousness and reflected consciousness.

UNREFLECTED consciousness is the consciousness of everyday life. I walk down the street heading for the street-car stop. I notice that the spring leaves are starting to come out on the trees; I see some attractive pedestrians; I gaze in the shop windows; I see a necktie that I like. Here the objects of my consciousness are the trees, the people, and the tie. Sartre says there is no "I" in this unreflected consciousness.

As I turn the corner, I am shocked to see that I have missed the street-car, which is disappearing down the tracks. I look at my watch and realize that I have forgotten to wind it **AGAIN**! I become angry with myself and thinking of my own stupidity. Now I am thinking about my own thinking. These thoughts about myself Sartre calls **REFLECTED** consciousness.

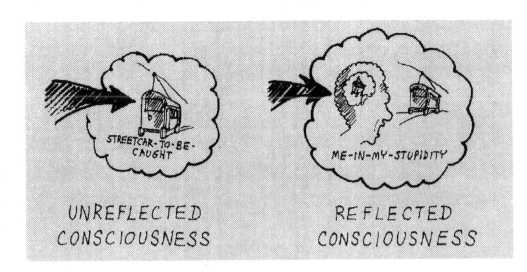

UNREFLECTED CONSCIOUSNESS

REFLECTED CONSCIOUSNESS

Here, the **SELF** can be found in consciousness, but <u>only</u> here, and only so long as I remain in reflected consciousness. The moment I am distracted again and I am back in unreflected consciousness, I am no longer aware of my <u>self</u>.

The point of this distinction is to show that Descartes was wrong, as was Husserl after him. The "I am" does not follow from the "I think." There is no self in thought except in reflected con- sciousness. But reflected consciousness is actually more rare than unreflected con- sciousness. Perhaps Descartes should have said, "I think, therefore there are thoughts."

Rather than finding an "absolute ego" in consciousness, as Husserl had done, Sartre finds an absent self. Consciousness, he says, is "an impersonal spontaneity," created _ex_ _nihilo_ (out of nothing), a tireless creation that overflows the self.

YOU DID IT!

EGO

ID

The self cannot cope with this "monstrous spontaneity," and searches for something like the Freudian unconscious to blame it on. But we do not need to invent an unconscious to explain these disruptions. They are parts of consciousness—but parts that we try to disguise from ourselves because they terrify us.

"In fact," suggests Sartre,

> "PERHAPS THE ESSENTIAL ROLE OF THE EGO IS TO MASK FROM CONSCIOUSNESS ITS VERY SPONTANEITY."

if this is so, it will prove to be very difficult for Sartre to characterize a truly authentic self - a self in "good faith" as he will call it.

To illuminate this feature of consciousness, Sartre tells us about a patient of the psychologist Pierre-Marie Janet: "A young bride was in terror, when her husband left her alone, of sitting at the window and summoning the passers-by like a prostitute." This young woman, perhaps angry at her new husband's inattention, may have thought to herself, "I can have any man I want simply by beckoning him from my window." She is terrified by the possibility that has just entered her mind—terrified that she might act on that possibility.

This "psychasthenic ailment," Sartre calls it, is actually only an exaggeration of the normal condition of the mind, because consciousness is "a vertigo of possibility," demonstrating that we are "monstrously free."

MONSTROUS FREEDOM

Think of the time you were driving at night in the rain on a narrow, dangerous road facing occasional oncoming traffic. One car coming at you has on its high beams. You "flash" your beams, but the other driver doesn't lower his. You are nearly blinded by his lights, and you are furious. As

he approaches you, you think, "I could drive right into the #!*¢¶§_." As you think this suicidal thought you suddenly grip the steering wheel hard. WHY? To prevent yourself from driving into him! You are experiencing "the vertigo of possibility"—your own "monstrous freedom" and you are terrified by it.

These ideas of Sartre's derive from a little book by the Danish philosopher **SØREN KIERKEGAARD** (1813-1855), called *The Concept of Anxiety*. Kierkegaard has been called "the Father of Existentialism," and he is one of Sartre's mentors, despite the discrepancy between Sartre's radical atheism and Kierkegaard's radical Christianity. Kierkegaard's book is meant to be a "psychological deliberation on original sin."

Kierkegaard imagines Adam in the Garden of Eden.

Even though he is innocent and happy, there is a slight shadow cast over his contentment. But he cannot detect the source of his disquietude. At last everything comes to a head when God commands Adam not to eat from the tree of knowledge. Perhaps it had not even crossed Adam's mind to do so, but once God prohibits him from doing it, Adam knows he <u>can</u> do it (that is, he is free to do it); and once he knows he can do it, he knows he MAY do it, and in fact that he probably WILL do it. So, for Kierkegaard "original sin" is simply the dread or anxiety of Adam when he confronts his own freedom—a dread each of us must experience when we confront <u>our</u> freedom.

DO NOT EAT THE FRUIT OF THIS TREE!

OK

BUT I WANNA

AND I'M PROBABLY GONNA

This theory is confirmed for Sartre by phenomenology, which also discovers that the anguish in the face of freedom is foundational to consciousness. Descartes believed himself to have discovered "the self" at the bottom of consciousness; Sartre finds only anguish.

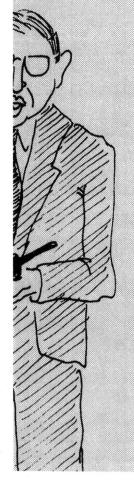

Edmund Husserl had seen the epoché as a philosophical tool for liberating consciousness from the constraints of practicality. Sartre believes it is much more than that. Sometimes consciousness liberates <u>itself</u> in an event that is a spontaneous epoché. Such a "bracketing" is not experienced with philosophical calm, however, but with something like terror. Perhaps in his novels Sartre is best at describing these experiences that we all suffer on occasion, but we try to marginalize them, ignore them, or forget them—a response that Sartre resists.

NAUSEA

In Sartre's novel of 1938, Nausea, his "hero," Roquentin, is riding on a trolley car. He is staring out the window across from him. Suddenly he loses the context of his situation as the buildings outside rather than the streetcar seem to be moving. This provokes an epoché-like experience that terrifies Roquentin. He rests his hand on the seat, but it feels alien to him. He feels not the seat, but its <u>existence.</u> He pulls his hand back hurriedly, he has to tell himself that it is a <u>seat</u>—that it was made for people to sit on. He tries to stabilize his experience with language. He says, "It's a seat.... But the word stays on my lips: it refuses to go and put itself on the thing."

Roquentin says that the seat that he is sitting on might just as well be the bloated belly of a dead donkey. Language has failed him. He says, "Things are divorced from their names.... I am in the midst of things, nameless things. Alone, without words, defenseless, they surround me, are beneath me, behind me, above me."

On another occasion in *Nausea*, Roquentin records in his diary an experience he had earlier while sitting on a park bench staring at the root of a chestnut tree:

> **66** Suddenly the veil is torn away, I have understood, I have seen.... The roots of the chestnut tree were sunk in the ground just under my bench–I couldn't remember it was a root anymore. The words had vanished and with them the significance of things, their methods of use, and the feeble points of reference which men have traced on their surface. I was sitting, stooping forward, head bowed, alone in front of this black, knotty mass, entirely beastly, which frightened me. Then I had this vision. It left me breathless. Never, until these last few days, had I understood the meaning of 'existence.' **99**

Before, says Roquentin, when he had used the verb "to be," it had designated nothing. When he had said, "The sea _is_ green," or, "That speck up there _is_ a seagull," the verb named an empty category.

Try this experiment to get Sartre's point:

Take a sheet of paper and draw "a seagull." Then draw "an existing seagull." They are identical! Therefore the term "existing" does not name a concept, an idea, the way "seagull" does.

SEAGULL

Concepts name what all members of a class have in common. Therefore, they are always

EXISTING SEAGULL

abstractions. But what Roquentin has discovered is that "existence" is not a concept. It is never abstract, but is always concrete.

THEREFORE BEING CANNOT BE THOUGHT; IT CAN ONLY BE ENCOUNTERED.

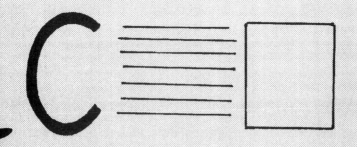

ake a look at this diagram. Let the open-ended figure "C" stand for conscious human experience, what Sartre calls **BEING-FOR-ITSELF.** Let the closed square stand for reality prior to any human intervention in it. This, Sartre calls **BEING-IN-ITSELF.** Between these two poles is "the world" as we know it—basically the world of humanly-created structures fashioned to deal with reality—particularly LANGUAGE, but also theories, explanations, institutions, mores, traditions and customs.

artre's view is that we never, or hardly ever, confront reality (Being-in-itself) directly, but only through the medium of human institutions, which in fact camouflage rather than reveal reality. Human thought is in fact usually <u>about</u> thought. It is a system of infinite self-referentiality, unequipped to refer beyond itself to real existence. It is for this reason that Sartre has Roquentin say that the word "existence" designates nothing.

Now, what has happened in the case of Roquentin is that "the world" of language, institutions, and justifications has suddenly collapsed as if sucked down a drain hole, and Roquentin, in this spontaneous epoché, suddenly confronts Being-in-itself, denuded of all artificial camouflage.

This is not a purely positive experience. Roquentin writes:

"And then all of a sudden, there it was, clear as day: existence had suddenly unveiled itself. It had lost the harmless look of an abstract category: it was the very paste of things...the diversity of things, their individuality, was only an appearance, a veneer. This veneer had melted, leaving soft, monstrous masses all in disorder—naked, in a frightful, obscene nakedness."

Sitting in his hotel room meditating on his experience in the park, Roquentin arrives at several philosophical insights. The first is the  **SUPERFLUITY** of all Being, including his own, which he suddenly experiences as "in excess," an unneeded addendum. But it is not just his own being that is superfluous— it is the <u>whole</u> of existence.

He writes:

"The word **ABSURDITY** is coming to life under my pen; a little while ago in the garden, I couldn't find it, but neither was I looking for it, I didn't need it: I thought without words, on things, with things.... In fact, all that I could grasp beyond that returns to this fundamental absurdity. Absurdity: another word. I struggle against words; down there I touched the thing."

This is not <u>relative</u> absurdity, but **ABSOLUTE** absurdity. (Most absurd things are absurd only relative to their context. A clown's antics are absurd in relation to the seriousness of everyday life. An absurd sentence is absurd only relative to the rest of language. But Being, as Roquentin has encountered it, is **ABSOLUTELY ABSURD**.)

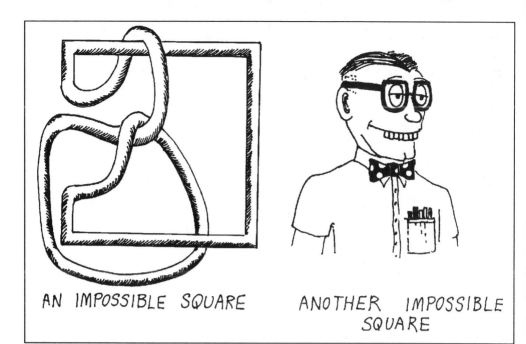

AN IMPOSSIBLE SQUARE

ANOTHER IMPOSSIBLE SQUARE

In his epoché, Roquentin has discovered the **CONTINGENCY** of all being. "Contingency" is the opposite of "necessity." The idea of a square having four equal sides is logically necessary. Any other idea of a square is logically impossible. But it is logically possible to conceive of the whole universe as empty. Now, in fact the universe is <u>not</u> empty, but that fact is a <u>contingent</u> fact.

This "contingency" of being—its "superfluousness," raises the metaphysical question posed so clearly by the seventeenth-century German rationalist philosopher **GOTTFRIED LEIBNIZ.**

> *WHY IS THERE SOMETHING RATHER THAN NOTHING?*

In order to answer his question, Leibniz had developed his "Principle of Sufficient Reason," which says, "For anything that exists, there must be some reason why it exists, and why it exists as it does."

For Leibniz, this principle was the criterion of rationality. Anybody who denies this principle simply declares himself to be irrational. So, take an example like the fact that my keys are on the table.

WHY
are they there? Because I placed them there.

WHY?
Because I plan to enter my locked office after writing this chapter.

WHY?
In order to pick-up my briefcase and go home.

WHY?
In order to... Again, every moment of being is explained by referring to some other moment of being on which the former is dependent.

And how far does this chain of explanation reach? For Leibniz, there are only two possibilities:

EITHER every chain of contingent being finally terminates in some NECESSARY being (a being which could not NOT exist—that is, a God), and that being anchors and is responsible for the meaning of all being ....

OR every chain of contingent being is infinite—in which case every state of being is explained by another state of being, which in turn is explained by yet another state of being, and so on <u>ad</u> <u>infinitum.</u> In this case, according to Leibniz, there is never any real explanation of anything, only infinite deferral of meaning...

and in that case, everything is utterly absurd.

Because the human mind cannot accept utter absurdity, Leibniz asserts that there must be a God who bestows meaning on the whole of the history of being. Without such meaning, life would be too horrible to bear.

Can the human mind deal with the idea of an absurd universe? Sartre believes that only the cowardly mind cannot do so, and he believes that such a mind posits God to relieve the anxiety provoked by the thought of a meaningless universe. But this belief is posited in "bad faith," according to Sartre.

> **ALL OF THIS IS WHAT ROQUENTIN HAS DISCOVERED IN THE PARK.**

Sartre's existentialism tries to reveal to human consciousness its strength and courage to accept the absurdity of existence, and its capacity for creating meaning in a meaningless world. Sartre develops these ideas in his massive work of 1943...
BEING AND NOTHINGNESS.

Phenomenology asks this question:

> **HOW DOES THE HUMAN BEING STAND IN RELATION TO THE WORLD?**

Taking his cue from the German philosopher MARTIN HEIDEGGER, Sartre asserts that this question contains its own answer—that is, the relation "Human-to-World" IS that of a question. In all of their actions, people pose questions to reality and are answered back "Yes" or "No."

When I sit on a chair, I am asking, "Will I be supported?" When reality answers "Yes," it reveals its "being" to us.

When it answers "No," it reveals its "non-being," its "nothingness." (Remember, the title of Sartre's main work is **Being and Nothingness**.)

Sartre explicates this idea by giving us a phenomenological account of arriving late at a café, where he has agreed to meet his friend, Pierre.

He describes the café as he enters:

"The café by itself with its patrons, its tables, its booths, its mirrors, its light, its smoky atmosphere, and the sounds of voices, rattling saucers, and footsteps which fill it," and he says, "the café is a fullness of being....we seem to have found fullness everywhere."

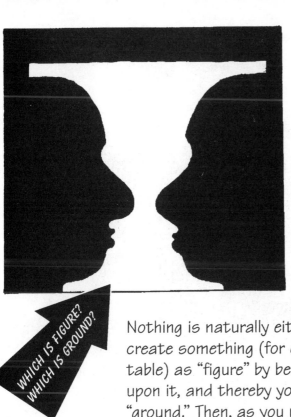

There is an important distinction in phenomenology between FIGURE and GROUND.

"Figure" is that feature of the field of perception on which you focus your attention.

"Ground" is the backdrop or foreground to "figure."

WHICH IS FIGURE? WHICH IS GROUND?

Nothing is naturally either figure or ground. You create something (for example, a glass on the table) as "figure" by bestowing your attention upon it, and thereby you create the table as "ground." Then, as you move your attention from the glass to a napkin, the napkin "leaps forward" as figure, and the glass slips into the ground.

Now, as Sartre scans the café for Pierre, different people and objects offer

ME!

No, ME!

themselves up as "figure," but each proves not to be Pierre, so they slide back into the "ground" as Sartre moves his attention to another part of the café.

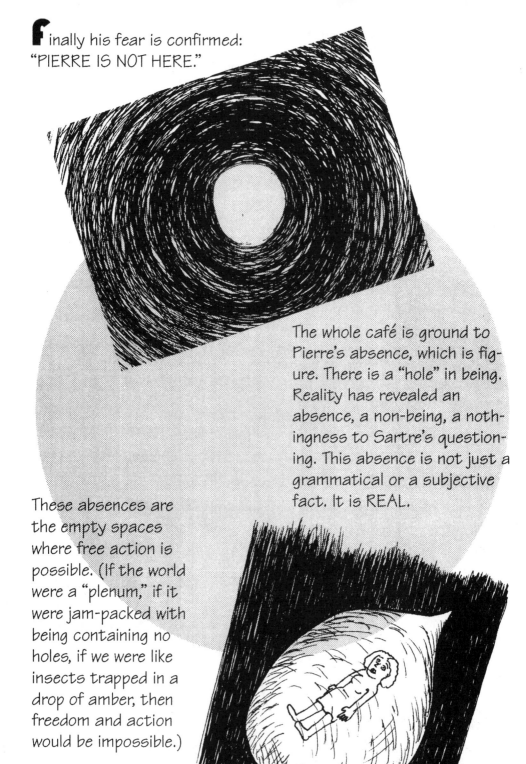

finally his fear is confirmed: "PIERRE IS NOT HERE."

The whole café is ground to Pierre's absence, which is figure. There is a "hole" in being. Reality has revealed an absence, a non-being, a nothingness to Sartre's questioning. This absence is not just a grammatical or a subjective fact. It is REAL.

These absences are the empty spaces where free action is possible. (If the world were a "plenum," if it were jam-packed with being containing no holes, if we were like insects trapped in a drop of amber, then freedom and action would be impossible.)

Both reality's "beings" and its "nothingnesses" become motives for human action. When I discover Pierre's absence, I must act upon that discovery and _do_ something, just as I would have to act upon the discovery of his presence. But ultimately it is non-being that makes all action possible, for it reveals the _discontinuities_ in causality, the holes in it.

Without these discontinuities there would only be universal DETERMINISM (every event would be rigidly caused by an earlier event, in turn caused by an earlier event, and so on to infinity), and no true action could exist, only reflexes, only effects.

NO JAM TODAY

As we saw, the phenomeno-logical epoché revealed that, in terms of "lived time," we exist in an eternal present.

(In Lewis Carroll's *Through the Looking Glass*, the Queen offers Alice a job with a salary of "jam every other day," then she tells Alice that she can't actually ever have the jam, even if she earns it. "It's jam every <u>other</u> day." The Queen declares, "Today isn't any <u>other</u> day, you know." Phenomenologically, she's right. It never <u>is</u> any other day. It's always today.)

But we experience the present as eternally flowing out of the past and into the future.

What is our relationship to these impossible places (the past and the future), according to Sartre?

Keep in mind that for the <u>determinist</u> there is a continuity of strict causality between the past and the present and between the present and the future. The past necessarilly causes the present, which in turn necessarily causes the future. Therefore, for the determinist, freedom is impossible.

For example, for Freud, an event in my childhood, whose memory is locked in my unconscious, can cause my neurotic behavior as an adult. Or for Skinner, all of our present acts are the effects of past conditioning.

CHOKES ON A PEACH PIT AT AGE TWO.....

I CAN'T STAND PEACHES! HOW DARE YOU OFFER ME ONE?

RSONDS AT AGE THIRTY TO THE OFFER OF A PEACH

Sartre denies all of this. Being-for-itself is separated from its past by a nothingness. It is true that the past has "FACTICITY." That is, there are certain facts in the past that one cannot change. (I, for example, was born in San Jose, California, and I can't do anything to change that fact—a heavy burden!) But nothing in the past can CAUSE me to do anything now. There is nothing that can be considered a human action (as opposed to reflexes or bodily functions) that follows necessarily from the past.

SEPARATED FROM MY PAST BY A NOTHINGNESS

To understand the sense in which FAC-TICITY cannot be the <u>cause</u> of any action, consider this Sartrean kind of example: A group of friends on vacation go for a day hike in the Alps. Halfway to the mountain top which is their goal, they turn a bend in the path and find their way blocked by a huge boulder that has fallen in such a manner that it cannot be dislodged and cannot be circumvented. The first hiker's stomach sinks in disappointment. "That's it," he says, "The hike's over!" From Sartre's point of view, this person has <u>chosen</u> the facticity of the boulder as an insurmountable obstacle and chosen himself as defeated. A second hiker begins photographing the rock, excited by its sublime power and by the beauty of the landscape framing it. She has chosen the boulder as aesthetic object and chosen herself as a recorder of beauty—that is, as an artist. A third hiker examines the boulder scientifically, noting its mineral composition and the impact of its recent fall on the path. For her, this boulder is a motive for scientific study and is the occasion for her to act as a scientist. The fourth hiker says, "There's got to be a way around this thing," and begins a series of experiments to overcome the obstacle.

> I GIVE UP!
> (LET'S EAT)

> HE HAS CHOSEN THE BOULDER'S FACTICITY AS A CHALLENGE AND HIMSELF AS HERO.

The determinist argues that there must be something in the past of each of these hikers that determined their response. Sartre denies this. There is nothing in the facticity of the past of any of the hikers, nor in the facticity of the boulder, that necessitates any particular response to the boulder's presence. For Sartre, the facticity of the rock is undeniable, but each person chooses the MEANING of that facticity for him or herself. Because facticity in itself is meaningless, the source of the meaning is a decision on the part of the individual. There are always alternative interpretations of meaning available; we are never confronted with only one possible choice. There is always the most radical choice of all—the choice of death. A hiker might decide that the boulder's presence is so depressing that he cannot go on living. This would of course be an ABSURD response to the boulder's facticity, but its mere possibility shows Sartre that all other responses were chosen as alternatives to death. If you did not kill yourself this morning (and apparently you didn't) then you chose an alternative to death... and you are responsible for that choice and for its consequences.

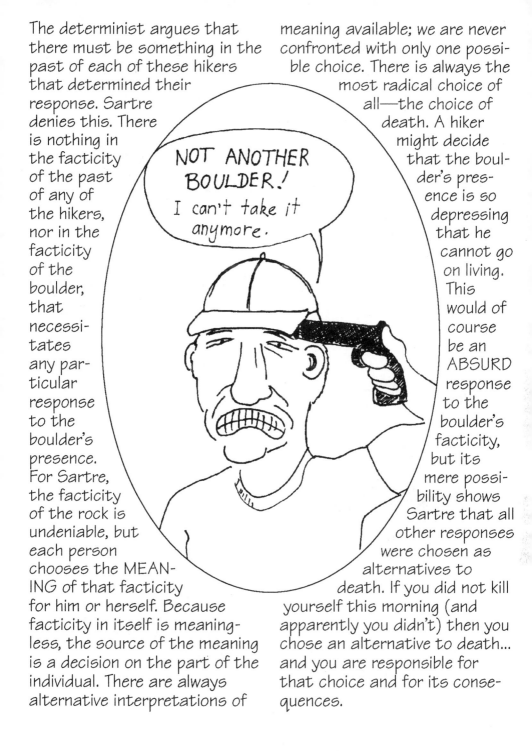

Let us now return to the human stance regarding the past.

THESE ARE THE MOST IMPORTANT THINGS ABOUT ME.

There is, as we said, facticity in our past (as there was in the boulder), but because there is nothingness between us and our past, the past cannot cause the present; we must determine the meaning our past has for us. If I am born with big feet (or born short, or in an Irish Catholic family, or with a stiff knee), it is I who decide the MEANING (of my "vertical challenge," or of my Irishness, or of my disability).

My big feet may prevent me from becoming a ballerina, and my Irishness may keep me from becoming a Watusi king, but the meaning of these facts, too, derives from me alone.

The self is related to its past somewhat the way nations are related to their past. Certain events (real or fictitious) are chosen as being definitional, are called "HISTORY," and are then incorporated into the present perhaps the way the state of Israel has treated the heroic suicidal stand of the Zealots against the Roman legions at Masada in the year 73 AD, or the way the French trace their nationhood to the Emperor Charlemagne (even though he was a German!). Americans choose the Gettysburg Address as definitional, or, more suspiciously, George Washington's inability to lie, or his ability to stand up in a rowboat while crossing the Delaware in a battle.

In fact, think of how much history is written in terms of Great River Crossings. (Caesar crossed the Rubicon, Attila crossed the Po, Charlemagne crossed the Ebro, Emperor Charles I crossed the Elbe, Patton crossed the Rhine.)

There is nothing particularly significant in a river crossing (any more than there would be in Great Steppings in Dog Poop); rather, the significance comes from the <u>symbolism</u> of these events. (Caesar's crossing the Rubicon stands for his defiance of the democratic government in Rome.) Calling an event symbolic is to imbue it with a meaning that goes beyond its mere facticity. It would be possible to ascribe <u>other</u> meanings to those events. (What if George Washington had lost the War of Independence? What if Charlemagne had converted to Islam? Caesar had drowned?) The same is true of the meaning individuals ascribe to their own past.

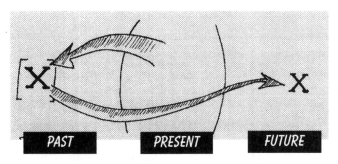

Then why is it that most people act in such predictable ways?

Why does the hiker who chose himself as defeated <u>always</u> throw in the towel early? Why does the "heroic" hiker see <u>all</u> obstacles as challenges? According to Sartre, most people choose an aspect of their past, then project it into the future as part of themselves, and then claim that because of this feature of their personality, they have no choice but to behave as they do.

> YA WANNA GO ON A DATE?

(I say to you, "I sure think Suzy is nice." You say, "Ask her to go to the movies with you." I say, "Naw, women don't like me." You insist. "Go on! Ask her! You've got nothing to lose." I reluctantly agree. "Hi Suzy," I say in a lackluster monotone, "Ya don't wanna go out, do ya?" When she declines, I say to you, "See? Women don't like me." Sartre calls this "BAD FAITH.")

Yet it is true that the past somehow seems to compel us.

THE PAST

Sartre talks of the gambler "who has freely and sincerely decided not to gamble anymore and who, when he approaches the gaming table, suddenly sees all his resolutions melt away." According to Sartre, it is not the case that this man's past is forcing him to gamble; to the contrary, the gambler faces a rupture with his past—with the past resolutions he has made and with the self that he was when he made them. A "nothingness" has come between him and his past. He experiences this nothingness as anguish.

The anguish that we can experience facing the future is even more extreme than that which we experience regarding the past—precisely because there is no facticity there. The future is yet to be constructed, and it is I who must construct it. Part of the anxiety derives from the realization that I am not now the self that I will be. As Sartre says, "I await myself in the future, where I make an appointment with myself on the other side of that hour, of that day, or of that month. Anguish is the fear of not finding myself at that appointment, of no longer even wishing to be there." Sartre's formula for our relation to the future is this: "I am the self which I will be, in the mode of not being it." This formula includes within it the nothingness that separates me from my future self. There is nothing I can do now that guarantees that my future self will obey the resolutions I make today or will hold the values to which I now subscribe. "Good faith" (and existential courage) must somehow involve a recognition that all of this is true, and a willingness to embrace this future and the anguish it entails.

I AWAIT MYSELF IN THE FUTURE.

ANGUISH

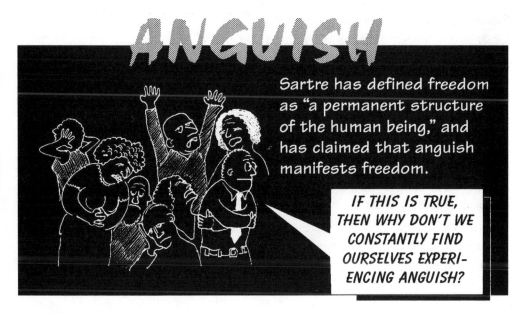

Sartre has defined freedom as "a permanent structure of the human being," and has claimed that anguish manifests freedom.

IF THIS IS TRUE, THEN WHY DON'T WE CONSTANTLY FIND OURSELVES EXPERIENCING ANGUISH?

Sartre admits that the actual <u>experience</u> of anguish is rare, and answers this question by explicating a typical early morning activity—that of responding to the ringing of the alarm clock. The ringing is the invitation to begin the day. It announces the possibility of <u>my</u> going to work, says Sartre. But I perceive it not as a possibility, rather as a necessity. I <u>must</u> get up, dress, eat, because I <u>must</u> earn the money to pay for the food I eat at breakfast so I can go to work. [!]

YOU ARE HEREBY INVITED TO COMMENCE YOUR DIURNAL PERAMBULATIONS

CHEE, TANKS!

Getting caught up in these "necessities" distracts me from the truth that none of this is really necessary except as relative to goals I choose.

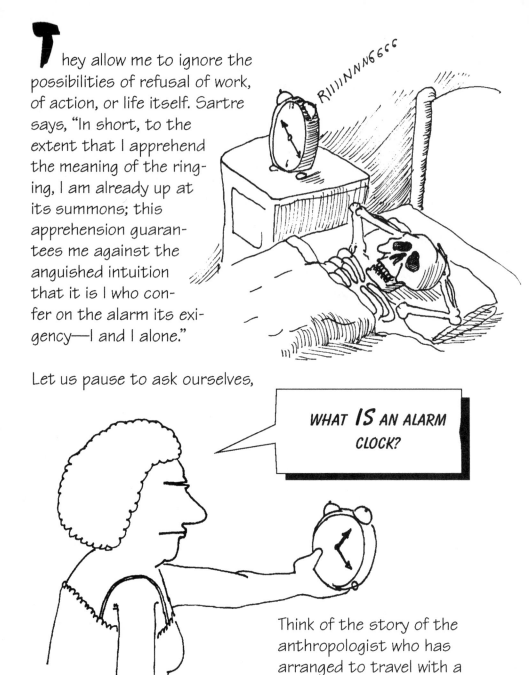

They allow me to ignore the possibilities of refusal of work, of action, or life itself. Sartre says, "In short, to the extent that I apprehend the meaning of the ringing, I am already up at its summons; this apprehension guarantees me against the anguished intuition that it is I who confer on the alarm its exigency—I and I alone."

Let us pause to ask ourselves,

WHAT **IS** AN ALARM CLOCK?

Think of the story of the anthropologist who has arranged to travel with a pygmy tribe through the Congolese rainforest. He must travel lightly, but he asks the pygmy chief for permission to take his Polaroid camera with him on the trek.

he chief has never seen a camera, so the anthropologist needs to explain it to him. He decides to demonstrate the camera's ability by taking the chief's picture and instructs the chief, "Stand there." This is a mistake. The chief takes offense. He is the CHIE, after all. A chief may tell others where to stand, but nobody tells the chief where to stand. The anthropologist apologizes, then makes his second mistake. He tells the chief to smile. But pygmies smile when they are happy, or when they find something funny. They do not smile when they are ordered to do so. Certainly pygmy <u>chiefs</u> don't do so.

SAY "CHEESE"

Finally, the anthropologist manages to take the picture. Triumphantly he shows it to the chief, but the pygmy seems relatively unimpressed. "What is it?" he asks. "It is you," says the anthropologist. Once again, the chief takes offense. The chief is not two-dimensional, four inches by four inches, detached from his body, surrounded by a white frame, smelling of chemicals. But the anthropologist persists. "<u>You</u> have two nostrils," he says, "and <u>this</u> has two nostrils. <u>You</u> have two eyes and <u>this</u> has two eyes. <u>You</u> have a chin; <u>it</u> has a chin." At last, the chief gets it. He sees the photo as a representation of himself.

Now he smiles. Then he asks, "What's it for?" The anthropologist tells us, "For a moment I could not remember."

And this is true. We are so accustomed to the role of photographs in our culture that we never question them. Most Americans, when asked what they would try to rescue from a fire, say they would salvage their photo albums. In explaining the value of photos to the chief, the anthropologist cannot appeal to passports or to drivers' licenses, for these do not exist among the pygmies. He says to him, "Photos help you to remember people you love." The chief is offended again. "I never forget anybody!" he says. —And the end of the story is that the anthropologist decides not to take his camera. He writes, "There are no cameras among the pygmies."

Similarly, there are no alarm clocks among the pygmies. So we can return to our question: WHAT IS AN ALARM CLOCK? It is a device for people who believe that they do not normally get up at the right time. But pygmies <u>DO</u> get up at the right time; only middle-class bourgeois set alarm clocks.

And this is the point!!

When you set your alarm clock you are putting into action and sustaining a whole set of middle class values. An alarm clock is what it is by virtue of being a part of a system of values. This system is sustained in being only by our CHOICE to sustain it. Anguish is the realization that there is no <u>necessity</u> in this system. We sustain it in being through our constant choices to do so. Sartre says, "there exist concretely alarm clocks, signs, tax forms, policemen—so many guardrails against anguish. But as soon as the undertaking is held

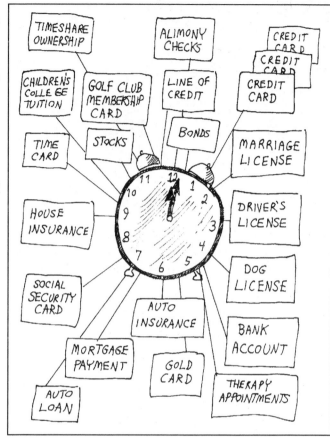

at a distance from me, as soon as I am referred to myself because I must await myself in the future, then I discover myself suddenly as the one who gives its meaning to the alarm clock,...the one who makes the values exist in order to determine his action by their demands." At this point, "all the guardrails collapse," destroyed by the consciousness of my freedom, and I experience the anguish of being the source of my own values.

VALUE

What is value? It is that which has worth, that which is desirable. We can find value in objects, in people, in movements (political or bowel), in ideas or in ideals. As ideals, values are motivations. If I value honesty, then I try to _be_ honest.

Plato held the view that Being is valuable in itself. (This is the exact opposite of Sartre, for whom, as we have seen, Being-in-itself has NO meaning, hence no value.) And for Plato, the purer Being is, the more valuable it is.

What is the SOURCE of value?

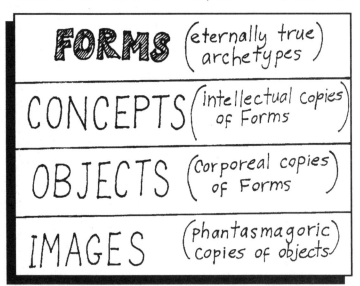

Plato believed that there is a hierarchy of Being, with that which is most real on the top, and that which is less real on the bottom.

In the Western theistic tradition too, Being, God's creation, has inherent value ("And God saw that it was good"); but God also allows in his creation at least the potential for negative value (sin, evil).

According to this view, positive value derives essentially from God, and negative value is the repudiation of that upon which God has bestowed positive value. This repudiation, itself sinful or evil, derives either from Satan—the Prince of Evil—or from human freedom or from some combination of the two.

AWESOME!

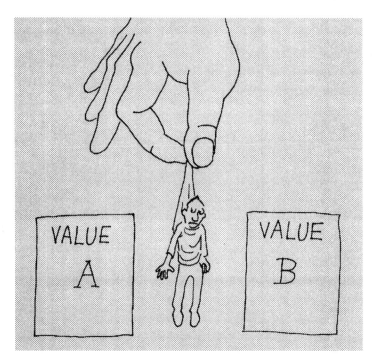

In this religious tradition the human being is created free, then set among values from which he or she must choose. But Sartre's theory is more radical. For him, there is no value existing prior to freedom. Value derives its reality from the fact that it is chosen rather than being chosen because it has value.

If I choose honesty, then honesty has value for me. If my behavior demonstrates that I chose dishonesty (even if I <u>claim</u> to prefer honesty), then I value dishonesty. ALL the values that guide my life exist only insofar as I have freely chosen them. The discovery of this truth provokes anguish. Sartre says, "As a being by whom values exist, I am unjustifiable. My freedom is anguished at being the foundation of values while itself without foundation."

Of course, many people claim to ground their values in some independent authority, such as in a national tradition, in a guru, or in God himself. But for Sartre, the Christian Søren Kierkegaard had already debunked that possibility. According to Kierkegaard, if I have accepted the Bible as the Word of God and as a guide for my life, then it is I in my freedom who authorize the Bible to guide me, and I am responsible for that authorization.

In his enigmatic little book **Fear and Trembling** (1843), Kierkegaard retells the Biblical story of Abraham and Isaac. When Abraham hears that terrible voice in the night telling him to take his son Isaac onto Mount Moriah and sacrifice him as a burnt offering, Abraham must decide for himself the meaning of that message. There are many alternatives open to him.

IT'S THE DEVIL TEMPTING ME. GOD WOULD NEVER ASK SUCH A THING. I MUST RESIST.

IT IS GOD, AND I WILL OBEY.

IT'S MY OWN SADISTIC NATURE SPEAKING TO ME FROM MY UNCONSCIOUS. I MUST RESIST.

I'M SURE I MISUNDERSTOOD. WOULD YOU MIND REPEATING THE ORDER?

IT IS GOD, BUT GOD IS A CRUEL MONSTER WHOM I CANNOT LOVE. I MUST RESIST.

IT MUST BE THE PASTRAMI BAGEL I ATE JUST BEFORE BEDTIME.

I HEREBY AUTHORIZE YOU TO BOSS ME AROUND!

KEEP OFF THE GRASS

But, according to Kierkegaard, when Abraham chooses to obey God's order, he is authorizing God to command him. God has not forced Abraham to do anything. (For Sartre, the same is true when we choose to obey a law, a policeman, or a sign.)

According to Kierkegaard and Sartre, when the Western religious tradition (Jews, Christians and Moslems) calls Abraham "the Father of us all," what that means is that we are all utterly free and totally responsible for our choice of values. For Kierkegaard, this thought provokes the "fear and trembling" of the title of his book, and for Sartre, it provokes anguish.

BAD FAITH

Most people flee anguish in "bad faith." In fact, bad faith is defined by Sartre as a flight from anguish, from freedom, and from responsibility. It involves a lie that one tells to oneself. When I tell a lie to someone, I hide the truth from her, but when I lie to myself, I hide the truth from me.

However, this is impossible, because I can't hide it from myself if I already possess it. So the project of bad faith is self-defeating. Nevertheless, that project is a central feature of human consciousness, according to Sartre.

Freudian psychoanalysis tries to explain how one can withhold information from oneself by dividing the self into a conscious aspect and an unconscious aspect, sometimes rendered as "ego" (Latin for "I") and "id" (Latin for "it.") Then there is supposed to be a censoring device between the two components, which does not allow me to know what is in my unconscious.

But, Sartre asks, on which side of the border is the censor? It can't be on the side of the id because it must censor the id. But if it is on the side of the ego, then the ego must know what it is censoring. That is to say, it KNOWS what it claims not to know.

SO FOR SARTRE, THE VERY IDEA OF THE UNCONSCIOUS IS ONE CON- CEIVED IN BAD FAITH. IT IS AN ATTEMPT TO MAKE AN EXCUSE FOR SOMETHING FOR WHICH THERE ARE NO EXCUSES.

Sartre illustrates the idea of "bad faith" by describing the case of a young woman out on a dinner date with a man she has only recently met. (You'll have to excuse Sartre if the example is anti- quated in terms of the relations between the sexes.)

HEY! I WROTE THAT PASSAGE IN 1942. OK?!

As the woman sits across the table from her companion, "she knows very well the intentions which [he] cherishes regarding her." She knows at some point she will have to make a decision concerning them, but she post- pones the decision because she does not want to feel its urgency. She wants to enjoy the moment.

When he says to her, "I find you so attractive," she "disarms this phrase of its sexual background." Sartre says she does this because she doesn't quite know what she wants.

She knows she inspires desire in her companion and would be disappointed if she didn't. But the desire "cruel and naked would humiliate and horrify her." She does not want to be merely the object of his sexual desire, but she does not want NOT to be the object of desire either.

Then her companion takes her hand. (The plot thickens.) Now she must make a decision. If she leaves her hand, that signifies romantic consent. But if she withdraws it, she breaks "the troubled and unstable harmony which gives the hour its charm." Her aim is to delay the decision as long as possible. Sartre says we KNOW what happens next. (Do we?)

She "leaves her hand there, but she <u>does not notice</u> that she is leaving it." She does not notice because she loses herself in her own spirituality as she hurries into a discussion of Life, <u>her</u> life as a pure personality. Sartre says: "The hand rests inert between the warm hands of her companion—neither consenting not resisting—a thing." Sartre concludes, "We shall say that this woman is in bad faith."

Why is she in bad faith? She denies his desire. She denies her desire. She denies her own body. There is a perfect divorce between her body and her "self." (Feminists want to know from Sartre whether he is willing to admit that the woman's companion is also in bad faith.) Sartre has a technical term to name this woman's mode of bad faith. He calls it "being-in-the-midst-of-the-world," that is, choosing oneself as "inert presence as a passive object among other objects." She has chosen her body as a THING, just as her companion has done. She does this to escape responsibility for her full self.

Another way we encounter bad faith is in our relationship to the social "roles" we play daily. When two human beings encounter each other they do so in terms of roles, which are formats of interaction that allow people to engage each other in efficient, non-threatening ways. There are professional roles, familial roles, political roles, entertainment and leisure-time roles, among others. There are even criminal roles. Almost any human act of which we can conceive has some rules curcumscribing it which must be learned by the "players" engaging in the act. Because people must interact with other people, there seems to be no alternative to role-playing.

Roles can enhance a certain kind of social freedom because there are rights and responsibilities attending them, but they also limit and disguise our more radical freedom, as they make it easier for us to objectify others and ourselves. Therefore they are unavoidably invitations to bad faith.

THE PURPOSE OF SOCIAL ROLES

In _Being and Nothingness_ Sartre begins his discussion of social roles by studying the movements of the waiter in the café where he is writing. (Pretty good life these existentialists have—always on a park bench or in a café.) Sartre says of him, "His movement is quick and forward, a little too precise, a little too rapid. He comes toward the patrons with a step a little too quick. He bends forward a little too eagerly; his voice, his eyes express an interest a little too solicitous for the order of the customer." What game is he playing?

THE GAME OF BEING A WAITER.

MONSIEUR CALLED?

I JUST CAN'T TAKE IT ANYMORE! SOB! SOB!

AUCTION TODAY

All professions have a similar obligation imposed on them. There is the "ceremony" or the "dance" of the grocer, the auctioneer, the tailor. The public demands of them that they undertake this ceremony in order to prove that they are <u>nothing but</u> a grocer, an auctioneer, a tailor. A grocer who dreams is offensive. We don't want an auctioneer who tells us about the messy divorce he is going through.

This demand is most obvious in the military, where the new soldier is instructed that he is not saluting the man, but the uniform. When the command "Eyes left!" is given when marching past the General's review stand, woe unto the soldier if his eyes actually make contact with the General's! (It may be difficult for young conscripts fresh from the farm to kill other young conscripts, but easier to kill other "uniforms.")

We are in bad faith when we try to turn the other person into a thing with our gaze (into "the waiter," "the tailor," "the auctioneer," "the soldier"), but these individuals can also put themselves in bad faith by trying to be nothing but their roles.

I VAS CHUST OBEYINK ORDERS

In fact, a waiter cannot BE a waiter in the sense that a rock is a rock, or an ashtray is an ashtray. That is, he cannot be it in the mode of being-in-itself. If I am a waiter, I am so in the mode of not-being-a-waiter. Being-for-itself can never become a THING, even if it wants to.

The issue here seems to be this: Although the grammar of the verb "to be" is identical in these two sentences—

"This is a waiter."

"This is a rock."

—in each instance the meaning of the verb is radically different. In the human case it cannot be part of a definition, for the being of the "for-itself" is always indefinable and incomplete, and even capable of self-cancellation. Therefore Sartre is able to characterize "good faith" (that is, authentic human existence) in a particularly perplexing formula:

A FREEDOM WHICH WILLS ITSELF FREEDOM IS IN FACT A BEING-WHICH-IS-NOT-WHAT-IT-IS AND WHICH-IS-WHAT-IT-IS-NOT, AND WHICH CHOOSES AS THE IDEAL OF BEING, BEING-WHAT-IT-IS-NOT AND NOT-BEING-WHAT-IT-IS!

SURE....

RIGHT....

Sincerity

I'M LIKE THAT

"Sincerity," Sartre claims, "is the antithesis of bad faith." So it would seem that striving for sincerity is "good faith," but this is not the case. To try to be sincere is to try to be what one is. But such an effort already presupposes that one IS WHAT ONE IS in the way that a rock is what it is. Therefore sincerity itself is in bad faith.

Sartre illustrates his point with the example of a man who is homosexual. He is confronted by an accuser who demands sincerity and honesty of him.

REMEMBER, IN 1942 WHEN I AM WRITING THIS, THE SOCIAL PRESSURES WOULD BE VERY STRONG FOR THE MAN TO REMAIN "IN THE CLOSET," EVEN IN PARIS—ESPECIALLY CONSIDERING THAT THE NAZIS OCCUPIED PARIS, AND THEIR POLICIES WERE AS HOMOPHOBIC AS THEY WERE ANTI-SEMITIC.

*f the homosexual will declare frankly, "I am a homosexual," either shamefully or defiantly, the accuser will be satisfied. Sartre asks, "Who is in bad faith? The homosexual or the champion of sincerity?" The homosexual resists making such an assertion. He is well aware of his sexual orientation, but he also knows that he is not a homosexual the way a rock is a rock. Yet that is what the champion of sincerity wants him to admit to being. Therefore this preacher of sincerity is in bad faith. For that reason, the gay man denies his homosexuality, so he, too, is in bad faith. Sartre suggests that the following answer might have been in good faith: "To the extent that a pattern of conduct is defined as the conduct of a homosexual and to the extent that I have adopted this conduct, I am a [homosexual]. But to the extent that human reality cannot be finally defined by patterns of conduct, I am not one." In this case he acknowledges that he is a homosexual "in the mode of not being it."

Other People

So far we have seen that according to Sartre "the self" is not a substantive entity that continues unchanged through time, nor can its absolute certainty be deduced from consciousness (as Descartes believed he had done with his "COGITO, ERGO SUM").

THERE IS ONE THING OF WHICH I AM TOTALLY CERTAIN...

I THINK, THEREFORE, I AM!!

.... I THINK,-....

SOB! I WAS SUCH A NICE GUY!! SOB!

Nor is the self simply the biological unity that is one's body, as some materialists believe. (For there is no such biological continuity. The cells that constituted you eight years ago are all dead.) The "self" is not something that you automatically acquire by virtue of having had human parents; rather, the self is an ongoing construction recreated in each moment through our choices.

But there is another more troubling side to the creation of self-hood, according to Sartre—one that is revealed to us in the confrontation with other people. He explains this feature of selfhood by giving a phenomenological description of such an encounter.

I am sitting on a park bench (again!). I see another person a few yards away. What does it mean to see the other person <u>as</u> a person and not as, for example, a puppet?

To see him as a puppet would be to see him as a thing among things (beside the benches, three yards from the lawn, etc.).

NO BIG DEAL

If he were a puppet, his appearance would not change my relation to the other objects around him. But to see him as a human being is to see space and objects organized around him. When the other person comes on the scene, his appearance <u>disintegrates</u> the relationships I had established with my immediate environment. Things group themselves spatially around him, and, says Sartre, his space is made with <u>my</u> space. This person has stolen my world from me.

It is as if "the world has a kind of drain hole in the middle of its being," and that drain hole is the Other. There is an "internal hemorrhage" as my world is drained into the world of the Other.

Phenomenologically, the appearance of the Other forces me to reinterpret my world. Before my seeing him, the grass, the paths, the benches were there "for me." Now they are there "for him." It is like that sudden reinterpretation that takes place when first you see the figure in a psychology text as a duck, then all at once as a rabbit.

If I have objectified the Other by looking at him, if I have turned him into my object, then why is he so threatening to me? Why does Sartre say,

HELL IS OTHER PEOPLE?

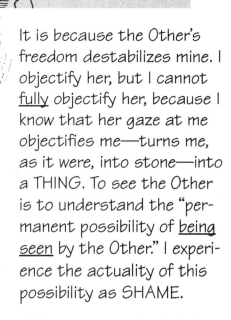

It is because the Other's freedom destabilizes mine. I objectify her, but I cannot fully objectify her, because I know that her gaze at me objectifies me—turns me, as it were, into stone—into a THING. To see the Other is to understand the "permanent possibility of being seen by the Other." I experience the actuality of this possibility as SHAME.

Remember the time you were talking to yourself when you thought you were alone, and suddenly you discovered that someone else was there observing you? What did you feel at the moment of this discovery? It was <u>shame.</u> Maybe you faked it, pretending that you were actually humming a tune, and you left, acting as casual as you could, without meeting the gaze of the Other.

AND WHAT ABOUT THE TIME YOU GOT CAUGHT PICKING YOUR NOSE?

GUILTY!

In shame we discover an aspect of our being which we would not have known otherwise. We discover ourselves as the object that is created by the Other's gaze. We discover what Sartre calls our "being-for-others." We are forced to pass judgment on ourselves as an object.

All of these common experiences (being slightly startled by the appearance of another person, getting caught talking to oneself or engaging in a slightly vulgar act) are minor versions of more dramatic episodes in which Sartre's point is perhaps more obvious.

I will imagine that, motivated by curiosity, jealousy or lust, I find myself peering through the keyhole of a hotel room observing the activities inside. The keyhole is both the instrument of my voyeurism and the obstacle that distances me from the action, which exists as the object of my "unreflective consciousness." My consciousness <u>just is</u> its objects and even though this consciousness is not disinterested and may experience itself indirectly in its jealous lustfulness, there is no selfhood or "ego" involved in my consciousness at all.

I AM AFTER ALL MERELY A THING

...AND A SUPERFLOUS ONE AT THAT

Suddenly I sense the presence of someone next to me. I look up and discover that the hotel detective is staring down at me. My self becomes fixed. I am made aware that the foundation of my self is outside myself. "I see myself because somebody sees me." I discover myself in shame. I am <u>responsible</u> for the self which has been revealed to me by the Other's gaze, but this self's grounding is outside me. In the moment of shame my freedom escapes me and the Other's freedom is revealed to me. I am forced to recognize myself not in my aspect of being-for-itself but in my aspect of being-in-itself.

Shame is not the only emotion engendered by the encounter with the Other. I can also experience fear. In fact, fear in its origin <u>just is</u> the discovery of my being-as-object. It shows me that my being-for-itself (where "I am my possibles") is transcended by possibles that are not <u>my</u> possibles. In fact, these feelings in their most exaggerated form may be the source of religion, according to Sartre. Shame before God is "the recognition of my being-an-object before a subject which can never become an object."

"God...is only the concept of the Other pushed to the limit."

If I choose myself in my shame, this is <u>masochism</u>, whose source is anxiety before the freedom of the Other. <u>Pride</u> is the opposite of shame; yet structurally pride and shame are similar. In both cases I recognize the Other as the one from whom my objectivity gets its being. When the Other sees me as beautiful, or strong, or intelligent, I accept myself proudly as being only that. Pride, then, is a form of bad faith, as is its close relative, <u>VANITY</u>. When I try to <u>affect</u> the Other with the objectivity she has bestowed upon me, this is <u>ARROGANCE</u>.

However, even in pride or arrogance, I have not recovered the self that I lost to the Other, for it is still her recognition of me that is the source of the meaning I attribute to myself.

The project of recovering myself as subject—that is, of recovering my freedom from its entrapment by the Other—necessarily puts me in conflict with the Other.

In fact, Sartre asserts, "Conflict is the original meaning of being-for-others." My project of recovering my own being assimilates the Other's freedom.

I can try to achieve this goal through <u>SADISM,</u> which is an extension of arrogance. In sadism, I use the objective being which the Other has bestowed upon me to make the Other humiliate herself. However, as long as the Sadist's victim can <u>look</u> at her torturer, the Sadist knows she failed.

NOT A CHANCE, BUSTER!

A basic way of trying to possess the free subjectivity of the Other is through sexual desire. Desire is an invitation to the Other's desire. Desire desires the desire of the Other. It is an attempt to reduce the Other to pure body, and to transform her into mere flesh <u>in her own eyes</u>. But desire necessarily fails, for either it <u>literally</u> fails to evoke the desire of the Other, or it <u>succeeds</u> in doing so, and then desire is absorbed in pleasure and loses sight of its original goal.

Rather than my desire transforming the Other into pure flesh, it transforms _me_ into pure flesh. Desire as a project, then, fails to recover the self that was lost to the Other.

All of this, of course, will make it extremely difficult to achieve selfhood in good faith, because every attempt seems destined to slip into its opposite—bad faith.

RESPONSIBILITY

um... ah, oh
FREEDOM
:cough:
FREEDOM
FREEDOM
and, er
FREEDOM
hem, ha
FREEDOM
(We're doing the
best we can
on that.)

Most people claim to want more freedom. They <u>demand</u> it. (Former President Reagan would mention freedom thirty times in a fourteen minute speech.)

Yet freedom is a burden.

WHICH IS WHY MOST PEOPLE FLEE IT IN BAD FAITH.

We are, Sartre says, CONDEMNED TO BE FREE. We carry the weight of the whole world on our shoulders because we are responsible for the world and for ourselves in it. Unless we lie to ourselves in bad faith, we are conscious of being the incontestable creators of our actions. And it is through our actions that there <u>is</u> a world—that there is a meaningful whole to experience. It is true that every one of our choices produces a "peculiar coefficient of adversity"—a resistance, an annoyance, a barrier, a problem. Yet we are the authors of this adversity too. Therefore, Sartre observes, "it is senseless to think of complaining since nothing alien has decided what we feel, what we live, or what we are."

A reminder!

According to Sartre, being-in-itself (reality as it is prior to any human intervention in it) has no meaning and no value. It just _is._ Meaning and value happen in the space between being-for-itself (conscious experience) and being-in-itself. Therefore, we humans are the creators of our world—of our "situation," as Sartre calls it. There are no non-human situations. Even the worst imaginable situations, such as war, are human situations. (Remember, Sartre wrote _Being and Nothingness_ during the Nazi occupation of Paris.) He says:

Even in its most dramatic moments, I have alternatives to it. I could desert, or commit suicide. But because I have _not_ done these things, I have _chosen_ this war.

Therefore, declares Sartre, <u>there</u> <u>are</u> <u>no</u> <u>innocent</u> <u>victims</u> <u>in war.</u> (This side of Sartre annoys many. It is as if in Sartre's world there are no animals, no children, no mentally deficient people. Everyone is a fully conscious, fully responsible adult.)
Sartre asserts,

QUIT CRYING! YOU CHOSE THIS WAR!

THE PECULIAR CHARACTER OF HUMAN REALITY IS THAT IT IS WITHOUT EXCUSE.

If you had to summarize existentialism in two words, they would be NO EXCUSES!

Some people respond grumpily to this line of reasoning, saying,

I DIDN'T ASK TO BE BORN, YA KNOW!

Sartre agrees that our birth is part of our facticity. Nevertheless, we have no choice but to take responsibility for the facticity of all of our "situations" (in this case, the facticity of our birth). We always have the option of negating it through self-destruction. Therefore, says Sartre, in a certain sense, we <u>choose</u> being born.

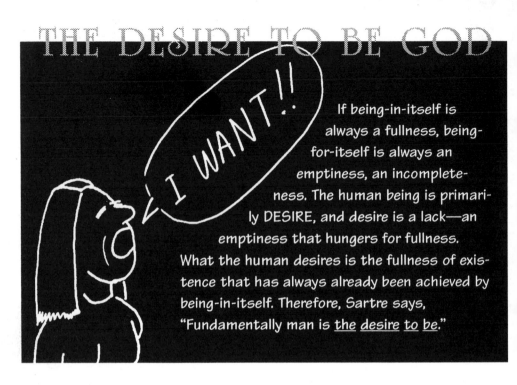

I WANT!!

If being-in-itself is always a fullness, being-for-itself is always an emptiness, an incompleteness. The human being is primarily DESIRE, and desire is a lack—an emptiness that hungers for fullness. What the human desires is the fullness of existence that has always already been achieved by being-in-itself. Therefore, Sartre says, "Fundamentally man is <u>the desire to be</u>."

Sartre does not mean that there is a primary drive called "The will-to-be" to which all other drives are reducible (the way Freud has "libido" as a primary drive); rather, the DESIRE TO BE exists <u>only</u> as the many forms of desire we experience (jealousy, greed, love of art, lust, interest in stamp collecting).

But, as we saw earlier in the case of sexual desire, desire can never be fully gratified. It can never fully achieve its goal. Or, to use Sartre's language, being-for-itself can never become being-in-itself. In fact, it does not really <u>want</u> to do so, for then it would fail to be itself (that is, fail to be "for-itself," a FREE-DOM). What it really wants is to be BEING-IN-ITSELF-FOR-ITSELF—that is, a freedom that is its own necessary source of being. But this is precisely the definition of God.

Therefore, "man is fundamentally the desire to be God." In every act we perform, according to Sartre, we are trying to become God.

(This is an ideal that Aristotle had introduced in the fourth century B.C.) The trouble is, <u>nobody</u> can become God, not even God. The idea of God is self-contradictory. (The idea of a being-in-itself- for-itself—that is, of a fullness which is an emptiness.)

HEY! I SAID IT FIRST.

Therefore, Sartre concludes:

THE SELF AS AN "ORIGINAL PROJECT."

Each individual's "desire to be" is, then, an attempt to solve the problem of the Absolute, and each individual's attempt is unique and constitutes an original choice of being-in-the-world. Sartre calls these choices "ORIGINAL PROJECTS" (or "fundamental," or "initial" projects).

Earlier we examined the cases of four hikers who confronted a boulder that blocked their progress. Let's review the example of the first hiker who threw down his backpack in defeat and sank into the grass, giving in to his fatigue and his disappointment. It was mentioned that this man probably <u>always</u> chooses himself as defeated. In fact, the determinists would argue that he has no freedom to choose any other option. Due to some traumatic event in his childhood (Freud), or to a history of conditioning (Skinner), he could not do otherwise than he does.

WHEN HE WAS A CHILD, HIS FATHER BEAT HIM AT MONOPOLY, AND HE NEVER RECOVERED.

I NEVER HAD A CHANCE

Sartre believes that the hiker <u>can</u> do otherwise—but doing so would not be a small thing in his case. Sartre poses the question of the man's freedom in this manner:

> COULD HE HAVE DONE OTHER-WISE WITHOUT MODIFYING HIS ORIGINAL PROJECT?

In other words, he could have done otherwise but, Sartre asks, "<u>at what price?</u>"

> I WANT TO **BE** HER!

> BUT I THOUGHT YOU SAID YOU WANTED TO BE GOD...

The price would be a "radical conversion of his being-in-the world." This RADICAL CONVERSION—which is <u>always possible</u> (here is where Sartre differs deeply from the determinists)—would amount to his choosing a new self; it would amount to choosing a new fundamental project, because the choice would manifest itself not only in that moment, but in hundreds of other ways.

For Sartre, the self is not a series of fragmented behaviors, but a TOTALITY. (Here he agrees with Freud.) The "original project" manifests itself in every act, big or small. But the original project is not equated with some event, decision, or fantasy in the past (here Sartre disagrees with Freud); rather, it is recreated at each moment through the choices we make and the actions we perform. And because the possibility of radical conversion always exists, we are responsible for what we are. This is like Nietzsche, who says that after a certain age a man is responsible for his face.

MAYBE THIS IS WHY SOME PEOPLE LOOK LIKE THEIR DOGS.

EXISTENTIAL PSYCHOANALYSIS

The phenomenological method Sartre devises for studying a person's "original project" is called "existential psychoanalysis." Its goal is to "discover the individual person in the initial project which constitutes him," or, in more detail, it will reveal...

...THE TOTALITY OF HIS IMPULSE TOWARD BEING, HIS ORIGINAL RELATION TO HIMSELF, TO THE WORLD, AND TO THE OTHER IN THE UNITY OF INTERNAL RELATIONS AND OF A FUNDAMENTAL PROJECT.

GOT THAT?

As has been noted, Sartre accepts Freud's view that the whole self can be manifested in a single gesture, that the self is a TOTALITY. He also accepts Freud's view that the individual is not in a privileged position to understand herself. However, Sartre's reason differs greatly from Freud's.

For Freud, the truth about me lies in my unconscious, which is distanced from me. Furthermore, I have unconscious resistances against this unconscious truth.

But, as we have seen, in *Being and Nothingness*, Sartre rejects the hypothesis of the unconscious as being a construction of theoretical bad faith. For him, as for Descartes,

> "the psychic act [is] co-extensive with consciousness,"

> and the notion of an "unconscious psychic act" is self-contradictory.

There is no hidden riddle. Everything is in consciousness, everything is luminous.

Nevertheless there can be a "mystery in broad daylight" because consciousness and knowledge are not necessarily the same thing. Reflected consciousness can provide understanding, but we must come to <u>know</u> what we understand. Following Plato, Sartre believes that experience can become knowledge only if it is correctly <u>conceptualized</u>. I can only understand my "initial project of being" if I can understand it in the light of its relationship to the being of others. (This is why the individual is not necessarily in a privileged position to know her own self.)

This means that existential psychoanalytic knowledge would be an understanding of the radical assimilation of "being-in-itself-for-itself" (that is, the attempt to <u>be</u> Being, or to be God) with "being-for-others." Existential psychoanalytic <u>self-</u>knowledge, then, involves a recognition of one's situation as being that of a freedom confronted with the freedom of others, of being in a necessarily conflictive relationship with others, and of recognizing one's responsibility for that situation, <u>and</u> a recognition of the freedom to "convert radically" from the specifics of that mode of being to another mode.

The individual goal of existential psychoanalysis, then, is not a "cure," as in Freud, but a grasping of one's self in all its possibilities. Not a freeing from the past, but an acknowledgment that this freedom always already exists.

EXISTENTIAL ETHICS

In philosophy, discussions of freedom and responsibility usually lead to the topic of ethics (that is, to philosophical theories of morality), including discourse about duty and obligation (what one <u>ought</u> to do). Yet Sartre's main existential work, *Being and Nothingness*, purports to be not an ethics, but an <u>ontology</u> (a theory of "being"). In other words, it is a description of what <u>is</u> the case, not a description of what ought to be the case. And Sartre accepts the formula of the eighteenth century Scottish philosopher DAVID HUME that...

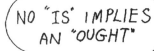

NO "IS" IMPLIES AN "OUGHT"

That is, a description of existing facts never logically entails a moral judgment. For example, take a look at the following valid syllogism:

1. Excessive pressure against human flesh causes pain.

2. Tom (who weighs 300 pounds) is applying excessive pressure against the flesh of Billy (a 40 pound two-year-old) by sitting on him..

3. Therefore, Tom is causing Billy pain.

But from that syllogism we cannot draw the following moral conclusion: THEREFORE, TOM'S ACT IS WRONG, <u>unless</u> we add a moral premise to the argument, such as:

"CAUSING GRATUITOUS PAIN IS WRONG."

The problem, according to Hume and Sartre, is that this moral premise cannot be derived from the mere description of facts; rather, it must be the product of philosophical argumentation, and Sartre knows that *Being and Nothingness* has not provided any such argument. (This despite the fact that Sartre's language of "bad faith" and "inauthenticity" seems morally loaded. It appears that to say that a person is in "bad faith" is to condemn him or her morally, but Sartre actually denies that the term is judgmental.)

YOU ARE IN BAD FAITH!

...BUT HEY, THAT'S ALL RIGHT! DIFFERENT STROKES FOR DIFFERENT FOLKS

In order to correct this deficit, at the end of *Being and Nothingess*, Sartre promised a book on ethics as a sequel to his ontology. Despite writing hundreds of pages of notes for such a book, Sartre eventually abandoned the project, having by then taken a new philosophical direction that would prevent him from producing an "existentialist ethics." (We will inspect this new turn of events shortly.) Nevertheless, in his essay of 1946, "Existentialism is a Humanism," he had some interesting things to say about ethics which sketch the outlines of what an existentialist ethics would be like.

In this essay, Sartre summarizes and simplifies his views in *Being and Nothingness*, saying:

TO CHOOSE THIS OR THAT IS TO AFFIRM AT THE SAME TIME THE VALUE OF WHAT WE CHOOSE, BECAUSE WE CAN NEVER CHOOSE EVIL. WE ALWAYS CHOOSE THE GOOD, AND NOTHING CAN BE GOOD FOR US WITHOUT BEING GOOD FOR ALL.

There are two claims being made here. The first is that whatever we <u>do</u>, we have chosen as being superior to all of its alternatives (otherwise we would have chosen one of those alternatives).

I'D RATHER BE PLAYING GOLF

LIAR!

$\mathbf{T}$he second claim is that it is impossible to choose exclusively for oneself. Or, as Sartre says, "In choosing myself, I choose man." WHY? Well, because there is a certain universal logic involved in value judgments, even if values are produced by freedom. Despite the typical misunderstanding of the logic of value judgments, they are in fact identical to other kinds of judgments.

For example, if I claim
(correctly or incorrectly)
that this figure
is a triangle,

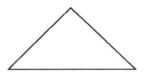

then I am logically committed
to claiming that this figure
is also a triangle.

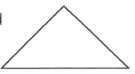

If I claim that the first is and the second isn't, I am "unclear on the concept;" I am contradicting myself. Similarly, if I claim that your walking off with my television set is theft, then I am logically committed to admitting that, all relevant features of the situation being identical, my walking off with your television set is theft. I cannot consistently claim that when you take mine it is theft, and when I take yours, I am simply redistributing the wealth.

THEFT

REDISTRIBUTION OF WEALTH

Putting both of these thoughts together, we come up with the idea that whatever I claim is good for <u>me</u>, I am logically committed to claiming is good for <u>all</u>.

Therefore, says Sartre, **"our responsibility is much greater than we might have supposed, because it involves all mankind."**

LYING IS GOOD

SHE'S LYING!

HE'S LYING!

SHE'S LYING!

HE'S LYING!

The only way of avoiding the jolting thought that every act we perform involves the whole of humankind is if we retreat into "bad faith," excusing our action by insisting, "Not everyone does that." But even this lie to oneself has universal value, and one puts oneself in the hypocritical position of holding the view, "Lying is good."

Now, this is almost precisely the ethical view of the German philosopher IMMANUEL KANT (1724-1804), who formulated his famous "categorical imperative" in the following words:

> SO ACT THAT THE MAXIM OF YOUR ACTION COULD BE WILLED AS A UNIVERSAL LAW.

Furthermore Kant, like Sartre, deduces from this principle that in desiring one's <u>own</u> freedom, one must desire the freedom of <u>all</u> human beings. So in a certain important sense, Sartre's "existential ethics" proves to be Kantian. But there are several significant differences. First, for Kant, the logical requirement that we will the freedom of the Other puts us all under a rule of universal law, while for Sartre, as we have seen, it puts us in a situation of irresolvable conflict. (Your freedom limits mine.)

> OF COURSE, I <u>WILL</u> YOUR FREEDOM, BUT I WILL MINE HARDER.

In fact, I may have to fight you in the name or your freedom. (If you use your freedom in support of fascism, I am obliged to fight you in the name of <u>both</u> of our freedoms.) The recognition of bad faith does not necessarily <u>prevent</u> bad faith.

Finally, for Sartre, even though logic enjoins me to consider the Other in each of my actions, logic cannot tell me what I ought to do in a <u>specific</u> situation. Sartre explains this point with a now-famous example of a student of his who came to him during the German occupation of France in World War II. The young man's older brother had been killed in an early battle; his father had become a collaborator. His mother, in despair over the brother's death and her husband's treason, depended totally on her remaining son for moral support.

The student was torn between his love for his mother and his loyalty to France (which included a desire for revenge against the Germans). He was torn between two kinds of ethics, one that put him in solidarity with the Free French forces preparing to join in the invasion of German-occupied Europe, and one that unified him with a single needy individual whom he loved. The first was more momentous, but abstract and less certain of success, the second more concrete but also perhaps more cowardly.

Which should he choose? Kant says:

You should act in such a way that your action could be a model for everyone else.

But <u>both</u> acts seem to be valid models of behavior. Kant also stated his "categorical imperative" in the following way: **SO ACT THAT YOU TREAT OTHERS AS AN END, AND NEVER MERELY AS MEANS.** (In other words, <u>don't</u> <u>use</u> <u>people.</u>) Fine! Except that either action he chooses risks treating someone as a means. He risks sacrificing his mother for the glory of France, or using the other patriots by allowing them to risk their lives for the recovery of his freedom.

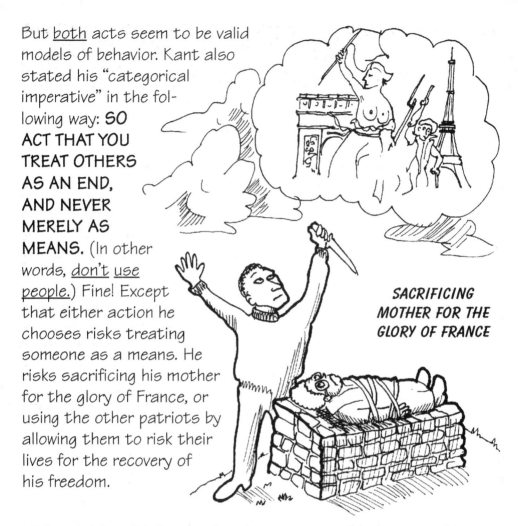

SACRIFICING MOTHER FOR THE GLORY OF FRANCE

What advice did Sartre give the young man? He says to him:

CHOOSE, THAT IS, INVENT!

In either case there will be anguish, but also the creation of a world!

MARXISM

Sartre had decided while in the German prison camp that after the war he would become more politically engaged. His political instincts had always moved him toward the Left and toward socialism.

I BELIEVED THAT ONLY "SOCIALIST MAN" IS TRULY HUMAN BECAUSE ONLY "SOCIALIST MAN" DOMINATES THINGS, WHILE IN OTHER REGIMES, THINGS DOMINATE "MAN."

In postwar France, it was the Communists who laid claim to the title of true socialists. But Sartre had always been suspicious of the French Communist Party, and of Marxism itself. The Party seemed rigid, inquisitional, and intellectually oppressive. Part of Sartre's annoyance with Marxism was its claim to have the status of a natural science. Science can study abstractions and external relations, but Sartre, as an old phenomenologist, thought that science could not study concrete human relations with their unique combination of subjective, objective, and historical features.

THINGS DOMINATING "MAN"

NEVERTHELESS, SARTRE BECAME MORE AND MORE ATTRACTED TO MARXISM (WHICH, HE THOUGHT, PROVIDED THE ONLY CORRECT ACCOUNT OF HISTORY) AND EVEN ATTRACTED TO THE FRENCH COMMUNIST PARTY (WHICH SEEMED TO HIM AFTER ALL TO BE THE ONLY VEHICLE OF UNITY AND EXPRESSION FOR THE FRENCH WORKING CLASS).

Despite his eventual "conversion" to Marxism, Sartre did not become wholly a Marxist because Marxism had "stopped." It had become reified (i.e., "thing-ified") and rigidified in its own nineteenth-century positivistic origins. It had claimed to find inexorable laws of human history; it denied human freedom; it treated social classes as independent <u>things</u> rather than recognizing that they are created by <u>individuals</u> with common interests; it treated society as a macro-organism that runs on its own.

MARXISM HAS BROKEN DOWN.

In fact, it was precisely phenomenological existentialism that could free
Marxism from its rigidity. Marxism
needs supplementing because in its
current form it cannot explain how a
specific individual of a specific class
chooses his or her specific destiny.
Marxism will not have an adequate
social philosophy until it can explain
both the weight of history on the
individual and the free practice of
individuals on the material and social
world—that is to say, until it can
explain the interplay of freedom and
necessity in human existence.

Sartre sets out to provide this marriage of existentialism and Marxism in his book, *Search For A Method* (1957), which served as the Preface to his two-volume *Critique of Dialectical Reason*, a work he left (typically) unfinished. The first volume was published in France in 1960, and the incomplete second volume was published in 1986, six years after his death. Even though there he demotes existentialism to a subordinate position to Marxism, he tries to humanize the Marxist dialectic by bringing existential insights to it. If the dialectic has become rigidified, the cure is to rethink the dialectic dialectically— but to think dialectically is to involve the subjectivity of the individual.

THE DIALECTIC

For Georg Hegel (1770-1831), from whom Karl Marx (1818-1883) had borrowed the notion, the term "DIALECTIC" was the name of the basic Law of Reality. For Hegel, Reality <u>is</u> history, and history is governed by Reason hidden behind the scenes.

CALL THAT REASON "GOD," IF YOU LIKE.

In fact Reality <u>is</u> the manifestation of Reason. However, Reason is not static. It moves ahead progressively toward an unseen goal of Unity.

It does so dialectically, that is, in terms of a THESIS (which is positive) that is opposed to but also dependent upon its own opposite called an ANTITHESIS (which is negative). The tension

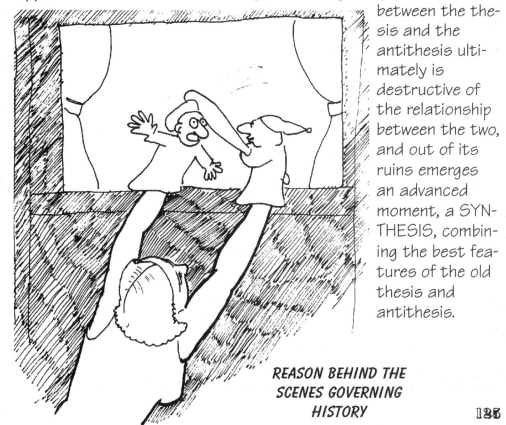

between the thesis and the antithesis ultimately is destructive of the relationship between the two, and out of its ruins emerges an advanced moment, a SYNTHESIS, combining the best features of the old thesis and antithesis.

REASON BEHIND THE SCENES GOVERNING HISTORY

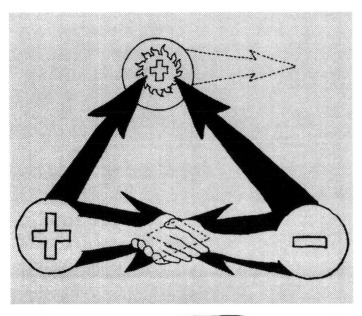

This synthesis (which is once again positive) becomes a new thesis, spawning its own opposite, a new antithesis; and the process of destruction, creation and progress continues. The Dialectic, then, for Hegel, is a law of history.

But the Dialectic is also the name of the mode of philosophical reasoning that Hegel utilizes and recommends. It is the mode of reasoning that grasps the rationality of human experience and history. It does so by discovering the positive in the negative, unity in plurality, freedom in determinism, totality in particularity. However, dialectical reason cannot affect history; it can only understand it after the fact. In this sense, dialectical reason is individual reasoning that grasps Reason after it has manifested itself.

DISCOVERING THE POSITIVE IN THE NEGATIVE

Marx "stood Hegel on his head." Human history for Marx was not the history of relationships between ideas, but of material relationships, particularly of relationships between social classes. "The history of the world hitherto," says the first line of *The Communist Manifesto*, "is the history of class conflict."

These social classes relate to each other dialectically being opposed to and dependent on each other at the same time. Ultimately the tension produces revolutionary conditions that overthrow the old social order, and move history closer to the most rational and human society, true communism.

However, history does not work itself out in terms of some abstract mental force called "Reason," but in terms of concrete material action on the social and natural worlds, what Marx calls "<u>praxis</u>." Unlike Hegel's dialectical reason, which can grasp history but not alter it, Marx's revolutionary praxis creates history.

In a certain sense, Sartre returns to Hegel.

Dialectical reason provides a way of understanding how human beings structure themselves historically, but it does not do so only from the point of view of the exterior of events, as does analytical, mathematical, scientific reasoning; it grasps them from the perspective of the agents themselves by finding the outer in the inner and the inner in the outer. In dialectical reason the subject discovers herself both in her freedom and in the necessity of her fate. She understands that her actions are her own and yet that they are alienated from her.

("Alienation" was one of the favorite topics of the young Marx, who was interested in the ways one's labor is snatched away from one by a hostile economic system and turned against one as an alien agent.) In dialectical reasoning she is able to say, "This is what I have done of my own free will, but this is not what I wanted." Here, as in Hegel, dialectical reason is the realization of a kind of "totalization," but one, as in Marx, that allows it to become part of revolutionary praxis. Thinking dialectically, for Sartre, does not simply happen after the fact, but is itself the motive for further praxis.

TOTALIZATION

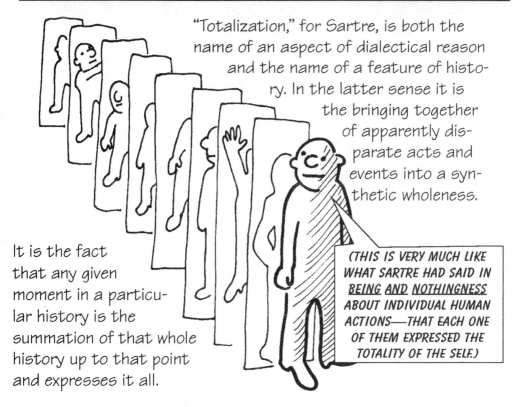

"Totalization," for Sartre, is both the name of an aspect of dialectical reason and the name of a feature of history. In the latter sense it is the bringing together of apparently disparate acts and events into a synthetic wholeness.

(THIS IS VERY MUCH LIKE WHAT SARTRE HAD SAID IN <u>BEING</u> AND <u>NOTHINGNESS</u> ABOUT INDIVIDUAL HUMAN ACTIONS—THAT EACH ONE OF THEM EXPRESSED THE TOTALITY OF THE SELF.)

It is the fact that any given moment in a particular history is the summation of that whole history up to that point and expresses it all.

In volume II of the *Critique*, Sartre develops this idea with the careful analysis of a boxing match staged in Paris sometime in

the 1950's. He will try to show how the individual praxis of each boxer derives from a larger historical totalization and how it adds to that totalization—that is, how it participates in the creation of history while being a product of history. This particular match only makes sense by being related to all other boxing matches everywhere, and in fact to boxing as a whole. It summarizes the whole of boxing by exemplifying its hierarchical structure and either confirming or modifying the particulars of that structure by producing a champ and a loser.

Using a religious term, Sartre says that each fight "incarnates" the whole of boxing. Indeed, he says that the match is the "public incarnation" of <u>all</u> conflict. In each fight the aboriginal motive is <u>scarcity</u>. In fact, for Sartre in his newfound Marxism, <u>all</u> violence derives from scarcity; therefore, this fight totalizes all violence. The general is present here in the particular.

COMPLICITY

And because boxing is the <u>public</u> incarnation of social violence, all the spectators are complicitous in it, as well as in the structure of exploitation that it also incarnates. Boxing is a capitalistic enterprise whose laborers are usually recruited from the working class. These young boxers have been formed in a violent world of scarcity, and they are enticed to turn their violence against each other. These exploited workers fight each other because they have not learned to fight their exploiters.

Then how do these two opposing figures unintentionally collaborate to move history ahead? Indeed, how do any two individuals or any two groups unintentionally cooperate to advance history? If there is no God, and there are no Laws of History to direct history and bestow meaning upon it, how can history have a meaning? Or, in Sartre's language,

It is this question that Sartre apparently was finally unable to answer, and perhaps it was this failure that caused him to abandon the *Critique*.

But he didn't fail for lack of trying!

And in his attempt he developed some interesting theories concerning the formation of social groups and the phenomenon of Stalinism in the U.S.S.R. We will finish our overview of Sartre's work by looking at these.

Sartre's phenomenological existentialism had adopted the position of Descartes' COGITO; that is, the perspective on the world from the point of view of the individual subject. Much of Sartre's earlier work had been an attempt to explain how an "I" was possible. But he had also asked the harder question, how is a "WE" possible?

In <u>Being and Nothingess</u> it was possible only through the objectification by Others. Sartre continues to develop this idea in the <u>Critique</u>.

COLLECTIVES

There are roughly three kinds of "we's" discussed by Sartre, three kinds of "collectives:" "series," "groups," and "the vestiges of groups."

(A) SERIES

A series is a collective that is created by some fact or force external to it. Sartre's most well-known case is one he observes as he sits at an outdoor table at the Café Deux

Maggots on the Boulevard St. Germain-des-Prés—a line of people waiting for a bus. What unifies them is the need for public transportation, namely, the bus. These people have no other "we-ness" than this need, and in fact have only a semi-awareness of each other.

Additional examples of seriality are people in different homes listening to the same radio broadcast, or all those people buying the same product in different stores. Their common denominator is an otherness that organizes the series, and in some of these cases the individual member may be totally unaware of the other members of the series. These kinds of collectives can be easily manipulated by the external force that organizes them.

(B) Groups

A genuine group has a common praxis that unites it. There are two kinds of these: the "fused group" and the "sworn group."

THE FUSED GROUP: When in 1789 the Parisian mob vented its rage against the King of France by storming the Bastille—a prison that was a hated symbol of oppression—they created a genuine "we," but it could last only as long as the passion that united them.

THE SWORN GROUP: A group may have gained its goal by vanquishing an enemy or overcoming an obstacle. But when the enemy or obstacle is gone, what holds them together? An OATH can create this solidarity. However, in taking an oath, I invite the group to punish or kill me if I break the oath, and therefore a new fear is introduced—not one coming in from outside, but fear of the group itself. This "we," then, is produced through terror.

The third kind of collective is
(C) VESTIGE OF A GROUP.

Here the group has lost its original motive, and the oath no longer has its original meaning. The group has sunk into a form of inertia that holds it together. A political party or a religion that has evolved away from the passion and radicalness of its messianic origins would be examples.

In fact, such a development is all too common, and in Sartre's most pessimistic moments he seemed to feel that this form of "sclerosis" was the most inevitable outcome of any social movement (including, perhaps, the Russian Revolution). "Praxis," whether engaged in by individuals or groups, is a reciprocal relationship between action and the material world, where action transforms the world, but is in turn somewhat transformed by the nature of the problem praxis is meant to solve.

Praxis is meant to dominate the material world, but it is not uncommon for the relation to be inverted, and then matter becomes alienated from the praxis and dominates it. Each praxis involves both chance and freedom, but it produces an institutional format that becomes what Sartre calls **"THE PRACTICO-INERT,"** that is, a historical weight that dictates future praxis. This "practico-inert," then, is meant to eliminate chance from praxis.

(For example, the formats for succession of monarchs and presidents is meant to eliminate the chance of civil war upon the death of national leaders.) But it also ends up limiting freedom, and in fact can enslave the agents of praxis. Furthermore, the "practico-inert" always produces some results that were unintended by the agents of the original praxis, and even ends up changing the agents themselves.

We see such a development taking place within the sworn group. The very nature of individual praxis within such a group is likely to produce different interpretations of the meaning of the oath and of the goals of the group. That is, subgroups are created. Each of the subgroups believes itself to be the true bearer of the group's interest, and each subgroup sees the praxis of the other subgroup as enemy action and a threat to the whole group, and each tries to expel or liquidate the other. In Sartre's view, contrary to those of Georg Hegel or Friedrich Engels (who represents "rigidified Marxism"), the Dialectic does not guarantee that the conflict between two subgroups will produce progress in history. There will be progress only if that conflict increases the effectiveness of the group at large. (Sartre is thinking of the divisions that developed during the French Revolution between subgroups like the Jacobins and the Girondins, and he is thinking of the opposition between Trotsky and Stalin in the aftermath of the Russian Revolution.)

OFF WITH THEIR HEADS!

In fact, a massive section of Volume II of the *Critique* is dedicated to an analysis of Stalin's rise to power and to addressing the question of whether

Stalinism represents historical progress or historical failure. Despite Sartre's generally sympathetic treatment of Stalin, he is unable to answer that question by the end of his book.)

THE RUSSIAN REVOLUTION AND STALINISM

The original Bolshevik Revolution tried to liberate the laboring masses so they could control their own labor. But the world into which the Revolution erupted was dangerous, being an enemy to radical change, and scarcity reigned in Russia. Therefore, before the revolutionary leaders could achieve their goal, they had to create the machinery of productivity. Russia had to be modernized. This meant that a generation of workers would have to be oppressed in the name of their own liberation. Provisional structures to implement this were created (the "practico-inert"), but these hierarchies of power inevitably became absorbed by the leaders who imposed them, changing the leaders, and necessarily diverting the Revolution from its original goals.

EXPLOITATION OF THE WORKER UNDER CAPITALISM

EXPLOITATION OF THE WORKER UNDER SOCIALISM

(For Sartre, Soviet oppression in the name of future humanity is better than capitalist oppression in the name of profit.) But the leaders themselves fell into subgroups. Stalin feared that the Revolution might fail by becoming too abstract and intellectual. Sartre says that Stalin, unlike Trotsky, lacked the education to appreciate the theoretical aspects of Marxism, but also, unlike Trotsky, who had spent his adult life exiled from Russia, Stalin was close to the Russian masses. Stalin's successful motto in his opposition to Trotsky was "SOCIALISM IN ONE COUNTRY." According to Sartre, this slogan was a "monstrosity" that constituted a deviation from the original goals of worldwide revolution, but it triumphed because the Revolution had to deviate or collapse.

It chose the detour of deviation, and "Stalin is the man of this detour." Stalin was not the

only possibility (Sartre never succumbs to "rigidified Marxism's" claim of historical necessity at the total expense of human freedom), but certain steps needed to be taken, and Stalin could take them better than anyone else.

Stalin made terrible errors—so terrible that Sartre wonders if Stalin really was the man history needed at that moment. Perhaps "the man history needed" simply didn't exist (just in the same way that such a man did not exist after the French Revolution, when history needed a man of peace, but got Napoleon).

Still, for better or for worse, Stalin became the Totalization of the Revolution. The result is that a very different Soviet Union was constructed from the one intended by the original revolutionaries. Writing after Stalin's death, Sartre wants to know whether the Revolution can now be rerouted toward its original goals, whether socialism in the Soviet Union can be saved from Stalinism.

Of course, <u>we</u> know the answer that Sartre could not have known then. We have seen the collapse of the U.S.S.R. and with it the apparent collapse of the Revolution. In fact, ten years after writing Volume II of the *Critique*, Sartre himself said:

...the machine cannot be repaired; the peoples of Eastern Europe must seize hold of it and destroy it.

His disappointment with the outcome of the Russian Revolution was reflected in his disappointment with the *Critique of Dialectical Reason* to which he had dedicated so much time. He told an interviewer in 1969, a year after the Soviet invasion of Czechoslovakia, that Volume II of the *Critique* would probably never appear. It did so only after his death and without his permission.

THE END

BIBLIOGRAPHY

I. <u>SARTRE'S MAIN WORKS IN ENGLISH TRANSLATION</u>.
Astericks indicate fiction or drama.

Emotions: Outline of a Theory. Trans. Bernard Frechtman. New York: Citadel Press, 1984. (*L'Imagination*. Paris: Presses Universitaires de France, 1936.)

The Transcendence of the Ego. Trans. Robert Kirkpatrick. New York: Farrar, Strauss and Giroux, 1957. (*La Transcendance de l'Ego*. Paris: Vrin, 1937.)

****Nausea.*** Trans. Lloyd Alexander. New York: New Directions, 1964. (*La Nausée*. Paris: Gallimard, 1938.)

Being and Nothingness. Trans. Hazel Barnes. New York: Washington Square Press, 1992. (*L'Etre et le Néant*. Paris: Gallimard, 1943.)

****The Flies***. Trans. Stuart Gilbert. New York: Alfred A. Knopf, 1962. (*Les Mouches*. Paris: Gallimard, 1943.)

****No Exit.*** Trans. Stuart Gilbert. New York: Vintage Book, 1947. (*Huis Clos*. Paris: Gallimard, 1944.)

****The Age of Reason.*** Trans. Eric Sutton. New York: Bantam Books, 1992. (*L'Age de rai-son*, Paris: Gallimard, 1945.)

****The Reprieve.*** Trans. Eric Sutton. New York: Bantam Books, 1964. (*Le Sursis*. Paris: Gallimard, 1945.)

Existentialism and Human Emotions. Trans. Bernard Frechtman and Hazel Barnes. New York: Citadel Press, 1977. (*L'Extentialisme est un humanisme*. Paris: Nagel, 1946.)

Anti-Semite and Jew. Trans. George J. Becker. New York: Schocken, 1974: (*Réflections sur la question juive*. Paris: Gallimard, 1946.)

Dirty Hands. Trans. Lionel Abel. New York: Alfred A. Knopf, 1949. (*Les Mains sales*. Paris: Gallimard, 1948.)

Saint Genêt: Actor and Martyr. Trans. Bernard Frechtman. New York: G. Braziller, 1963. *Saint Genêt, comédien et martyr.* Paris: Gallimard, 1952.)

Search for a Method. Trans. Hael Barnes. New York: Vintage Books, 1968. ("Questions de Méthode," preface to *Critique de la raison dialectique,* Tome I. Paris: Gallimard, 1960.)

Critique of Dialectical Reason, Vol.I: *Theory of Practical Ensembles.* Trans. Alan Sheridan Smith. London, Routledge, Chapman and Hall, 1984. (*Critique de la raison dialectique,* Tome I: *Théories des ensembles practiques.* Paris: Gallimard, 1960. Also, Tome II [inachevé]: *L' Intelligibilité de l' historie, etablissement du texte, notes et glossaire par Arlette Elkaïme-Sartre.* Paris: Gallimard, 1985. No English translation yet available.)

The Idiot of the Family. Trans. Carol Cosman. Chicago: University of Chicago Press, Vol. I, 1981; Vol. II, 1987; Vol. III, 1989. (*L'Idiot de la famille.* Paris: Gallimard, 1971.)

Notebooks for an Ethics. Trans. David Pellauer. Chicago: University of Chicago Press, 1992. (*Cahiers pour une morale.* Paris: Gallimard, 1983.)

Troubled Sleep. Trans. Gerard Hopkins. New York: Bantam Books, 1964. (*La Mort dans l'âme.* Paris: Gallimard, 1949.)

II. SARTRE'S PHILOSOPHY ANTHOLOGIZED.

The Philosophy of Jean-Paul Sartre. Ed. Robert Denoon Cumming. New York: Vintage Books, 1972.

III. RECOMMENDED SECONDARY SOURCES.

Aronson, Ronald. *Sartre's Second Critique.* Chicago: The University of Chicago Press, 1987.

Catalno, Joseph S. *A Commentary on Jean-Paul Sartre's "Being and Nothingness."* Chicago: The University of Chicago Press, 1980.

Caws, Peter, *Sartre.* Boston: Routledge and Kegan Paul, 1979.

Danto, Arthur C. *Jean-Paul Sartre.* New York: Viking Press, 1975.

De Beauvoir, Simone. *The Ethics of Ambiguity.* Trans. Bernard Frechtman. New York: Philosophical Library, 1948.

Hayman, Ronald. *Sartre: A Biography.* New York: Simon and Schuster, 1987.

La Capra, Dominick, *A Preface to Sartre,* Ithaca, New York: Cornell University Press, 1978.

Murdoch, Iris. *Sartre: Romantic Rationalist.* New York: Viking Press, 1987.

Sheridan, James F., Jr. *Sartre: The Radical Conversion.* Athens, Ohio: Ohio University Press, 1969.

Warnock, Mary, ed. *Sartre: A Collection of Critical Essays.* Garden City, New York: Anchor Books, 1971.

SOURCES OF QUOTED PASSAGES

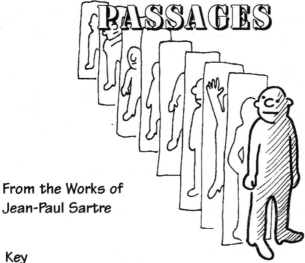

**From the Works of
Jean-Paul Sartre**

Key

BN = *Being and Nothingness.* Trans. Hazel Barnes. New York: Washington Square Press, 1992.

EHE = *Existentialism and Human Emotions.* Trans. Bernard Frechtman and Hazel Barnes. New York: Citadel Press, 1977.

N = *Nausea.* Trans. Lloyd Alexander. New York: New Directions, 1964.

TE = *Transcendence of the Ego.* Trans. Robert Kirkpatrick. New York: Farrar, Strauss and Giroux, 1957.

The left column designates page numbers from *Sartre for Beginners.* The right column designates page numbers from Sartre's works keyed above. First and last words from each quotation are listed.

GLOSSARY

(An asterisk* marks terms that can be cross-referenced in the glossary.)

ABANDONMENT. Sartre's term designating the consequence of individuation. A sensation of metaphysical isolation according to which each individual subject must ultimately fall back on its own resources.

ABSURDITY. Sartre's term for the fact that nothing can rationalize existence. Nothing in or beyond being can explain being's prescence.

AGNOSTICISM. Deriving from the Greek term for ignorance. The claim that we do not or cannot know whether God exists.

AGREGATION. An examination in the French academic system. Those who pass it are given the top ranking in the competition for jobs in higher education.

ALIENATION. A term in the theories of G.W.F. Hegel (1770-1831) and Karl Marx (1818-1883) designating a state of divided selfhood in which one is distanced from one's true being and confronts one's own self as an alien being.

ANGUISH. The vertiginous sensation of groundlessness experienced when the contingency* or freedom* of action reveals itself to consciousness.

ATHEISM. The denial of, or disbelief in, the existence of a supreme being, God.

BAD FAITH. Sartre's term for self-deception, the paradoxical state of lying to oneself, involving an impossible attempt at a flight from freedom, responsibility and anguish.

BEING-FOR-ITSELF. Sartre's name for exclusively human existence—a form of consciousness which is open-ended to the past, present and future. A form of consciousness that entertains itself as possibility rather than as terminal fact.

BEING-FOR-OTHERS. When I discover that the gaze of the other has transformed me into his or her object, I have discovered my "being-for-others."

BEING-IN-ITSELF. Sartre's name for non-human reality as it is prior to human intervention in it.

BEING-IN-ITSELF-FOR-ITSELF. An impossible form of being usually attributed to God. A fullness of being and at the same time an emptiness waiting to be filled; a complete determinism* and a complete freedom.*

BEING-IN-THE-MIDST-OF-THE-WORLD. The form of bad faith* in which one chooses oneself merely as inert presence, as a "thing" among other things, as "being-in-itself"* rather than as "being-for-itself."*

BEING-IN-THE-WORLD. The mode of choosing ourselves as real beings, manifested in our actions, thoughts, beliefs, aspirations and meanings.

BRACKETING. See "EPOCHÉ."

CATEGORICAL IMPERATIVE. Immanuel Kant's (1724-1804) principal moral commandment enjoining humans to perform only those actions that could be "universalized" (that is, performed by every person without contradiction). From this it followed, Kant believed, that it was immoral to use others for our own designs without taking their humanity into consideration.

CAUSALITY. A term designating relationships of cause and effect between events, where the cause necessarily* produces the effect. Determinists* assert that only causality exists.

COGITO ERGO SUM. Latin for "I think, therefore I am," the centerpiece of the philosophy of René Descartes (1596-1650), according to which this proposition establishes the absolute certainty required as foundation for the construction of a correct theory of knowledge.

COLD WAR, THE. The political, economic and philosophical antagonism developed between the Western capitalistic states (American and European) and the Soviet Union and its satellites after the termination of World War II.

COLLECTIVE. Sartre's term for any organization capable of grounding the concept of a plurality of unified individuals; i.e., the concept "we."

COMMUNISM. The form of socialism* advocated by Karl Marx (1818-1883) which equates the destiny of the human race with the destiny of the working class, whose interests will eventually triumph due to the mechanics of the dialectical* laws of history, producing the abolition of private property, and liberating humankind from scarcity, exploitation and alienation.*

CONCEPTS. General ideas that represent that which all members of a class have in common – an idea designating an essence.

CONTINGENCY. The opposite of necessity,* a term covering both randomness and freedom.*

DETERMINISM. The view that only necessity* exists. Usually, the view that there is no freedom,* or if freedom exists, it must be defined in such a way as to be compatible with necessity.

DIALECTIC, THE. A term in the social theory of Karl Marx (1818-1883), borrowed from the philosophy of G.W.F. Hegel (1770-1831) and modified to designate the fact that history progresses by resolving the contradictions between the opposing forces that make up any historical period (theses and antitheses) through revolutionary action (a synthesis). Also, in both Hegel and Marx, a scientific methodology in which socio-historical facts are analyzed in terms of their relationships of opposition to and dependency upon other socio-historical facts.

EGO, THE. In Freudian psychoanalysis,* the name of the rational, mostly conscious, social aspect of the psyche, as contrasted with the "id"* and the "superego." Also, a term sometimes used by Sartre, interchangeable with the terms "self," "I," and "me."

EPOCHÉ. A term in the phenomenology* of Edmund Husserl (1859-1938) designating the act of suspending all normal criteria of interpretation and judgement of psychical phenomena in order to inspect the actual structure and content of those phenomena prior to their interpretation.

ESSENCE. That characteristic (or set of characteristics) that an object has in common with similar objects, and which allows members of a class of objects to be defined.

EXISTENTIALISM. The term coined by Sartre to name a philosophical position derived partially from the nineteenth century philosophers S. Kierkegaard (1813-1855) and F. Nietzsche (1844-1900), according to which "existence precedes essence."* This view entails the assertion that there is no such thing as "human nature" if that phrase is meant to designate characteristics that determine our behavior. Rather, the determinant of our actions is our freedom.*

EXISTENTIAL PSYCHOANALYSIS.* Sartre's adaptation of psychoanalytic* principles to his own existentialism,* rejecting the Freudian concept of the unconscious,* and replacing it with the idea of "bad faith,"* the search for the "original project"* of the analysand.

FACTICITY. Those features of being-in-itself* about which being-for-itself* can do nothing. Those features of reality that resist freedom's* desire to transform them into possibility.

FIGURE. A term from phenomenological* theory of perception, designating those features of consciousness created by "attention" and "focus." The opposite of "ground."*

FREEDOM. A "free" action is one for which the necessary* and sufficient conditions of that action do not exist in the events preceding the action, rather the action is the product of a decision among genuine alternatives.

FUNDAMENTAL PROJECT. See "ORIGINAL PROJECT."

FUSED GROUP. Sartre's term for a "collective"* organized by a spontaneous common social goal or aspiration.

GROUND. A phenomenological* term designating the opposite of "figure."* That which serves as the backdrop of figure and makes it possible.

HOMOPHOBIA. The fear of homosexuality, and consequent hatred of it.

ID. In Freudian psychoanalysis,* the name given to the mostly unconscious* anti-social, "animal" self, containing the primitive sexual and aggressive drives.

INCARNATION. Sartre's term designating the fact that "universals," having no existence of their own, exist only in particular manifestations (e.g., there is no such thing as Boxing in general, yet each particular boxing match exhibits the features of all boxing matches.).

INITIAL PROJECT. See "ORIGINAL PROJECT."

MARXISM. The philosophical, sociological, and political stance of the followers of Karl Marx (1818-1883), according to which (a) human beings are the products of their socio-economic history, (b) that history follows the laws of the "dialectic"* (i.e., class warfare), and (c) the paradoxical outcome of economic history is the liberation from economic history, and the advent of true socialism.*

NECESSARY BEING. A being that could not <u>not</u> exist, a being whose non-existence would entail a logical self-contradiction. The rationalists'* conception of God.

NECESSITY. The relation in logic of strict entailment, or in ontology,* of strict causality. (If X entails or causes Y, then Y cannot fail to be the case if X is the case.)

NEUROSIS. A term from psychoanalysis* designating a kind of unconscious mental conflict that produces for the agent, a painful and self-destructive but nevertheless pleasurable "solution" to an emotional or psychological conflict.

NON-BEING. See "NOTHINGNESS."

NOTHINGNESS. The absence of being, a hole in being, a space of non-existence whose very "being" allows for possibility, i.e., allows for freedom.*

ONTOLOGY. Theory of being, theory of reality.

ORIGINAL PROJECT. The fundamental choice of " being-in-the-world"* that each of us makes in every action that we perform.

PHENOMENOLOGICAL SUSPENSION. See "EPOCHÉ."

PHENOMENOLOGY. Literally, " the study of appearances," but in the philosophy of Edmund Husserl (1859-1938), a method of analyzing the structure and content of consciousness, leading to the conclusion that such an analysis must be prior to and involved in the analysis of any other human endeavor (such as the practice of "common sense," science or art).

PLENUM. A fullness of being; being with no nothingness.*

POST-STRUCTURALISM. A radicalization of the theory of structuralism,* according to which the "structures" discovered by the structuralist theorists prove to be unstable and shifting, in such a way that the universalism of structuralism is reduced to a form of extreme relativism.

PRACTICO-INERT, THE. Sartre's term for the byproduct of any praxis,* which in turn becomes a precedent, a formulaic format for future praxis, and therefore both promotes that praxis, and also limits its spontaneity and creativity.

PRAXIS. Karl Marx's (1818-1883) name for human action, which for him is a form of creativity in which people express their productive potential (unless the process is subverted through the alienation* of labor).

PRINCIPLE OF SUFFICIENT REASON, THE. The principle of rationality in the philosophy of Gottfried Leibniz (1646-1716), according to which there exists the logical possibility of demonstrating the <u>reason</u> (cause or explanation) for every event or fact in existence. The opposite of "absurdity."*

PSYCHOANALYSIS. The name of the theory of Sigmund Freud (1856-1939) that studies individuals and cultures by explaining mental and social phenomena in terms of the dynamics between the unconscious* and the conscious mind. Also the name of the psychotheraphy based on that theory.

PURE EGO. The term in the phenomenology* of Edmund Husserl (1859-1938) designating the ultimate subject that performs the "epoché."*

RADICAL CONVERSION. The permanent possibility that each of us has in each moment of our lives of rejecting our "original project"* for a different form of "being-in-the-world."*

RATIONALISM. The philosophical view that (a) everything in reality is logically consistent with everything else in reality, and (b) the view that this logical consistency can be grasped by the human mind, because (c) the human mind reflects the logical structure of reality.

REFLECTED CONSCIOUSNESS. Thoughts about thoughts. A philosophical mode of consciousness.

SERIES. Sartre's term for a "collective"* organized by some common need that unifies a group artificially, but does not provide a genuine common social aspiration.

SITUATION. The individual instances of the world that is created by the free choices and actions of "being-for-itself."*

SOCIALISM. The political view (shared by Karl Marx [1818-1883] and Jean-Paul Sartre, among others) according to which the wealth of a society is the product of a common social effort and must be distributed fairly among all social agents in a manner recognizing the common effort of all.

STRUCTURALISM. A conception of social reality according to which the <u>content</u> of social meanings is reduced to the <u>structure</u> of social relationships. Associated primarily with Claude Lévi-Strauss (b. 1908), the French anthropologist, who coined the term.

SUPERFLUITY (or SUPERFLUOUSNESS). Sartre's term designating the excessiveness, the lack of necessity* of all being.

SWORN GROUP. THE. Sartre's term for a collective* organized by a specific commitment or a contractual agreement.

SYLLOGISM. A form of logical argument first identified by Aristotle (384-322 B.C.), wherein a conclusion follows necessarily from two premises.

THEISM. The belief in or claim to knowledge of the existence of a supreme being, God.

THEORETICAL ENTITIES. Posited beings which cannot be "constructed" from nor reduced to observable facts, yet are parts of theories whose function is to rationalize observable facts (e.g., "electrons," which cannot be observed, but which, if they had the properties ascribed to them, would explain certain factual data which will be otherwise unexplained).

TOTALIZATION. Sartre's term for (a) the fact that every historical moment is a product of and contains traces of all the moments leading up to it, and (b) the feature of dialectical* reason that acknowledges and understands events in terms of their relationship to all the other events and processes involved in them.

TRANSCENDENCE. A mental act in which consciousness projects itself beyond itself, refers to and establishes relations with entities that are other than itself. Or, human activity, which projects being-for-itself* beyond itself.

UNCONSCIOUS, THE. A term from psychoanalysis* designating desires, impulses, and intentions that motivate the individual but which are unknown or misunderstood by the individual.

UNREFLECTED CONSCIOUSNESS. Consciousness that has as its object something other than itself (e.g., thoughts about a tree, rather than thoughts about thinking about a tree). Our normal, everyday, practical mode of consciousness.

INDEX

I'M LIKE THAT

WITHDRAWN
Short Loan Collection